HOW TO BE AN E
GOV

In this Series

Other titles in preparation

BE AN EFFECTIVE
SCHOOL GOVERNOR

A practical handbook for parents

Polly Bird

Second Edition

'So how much extra income will they bring?'

How To Books

Author's dedication
This book is dedicated to the Governors of Grove Vale Primary School, past, present and future.

British Library Cataloguing in Publication Data
A catalogue record for this book is available from the British Library.

Consultant Editor Roland Seymour

© Copyright 1991 and 1995 by Polly Bird
Published by How To Books Ltd, Plymbridge House,
Estover Road, Plymouth PL6 7PZ, United Kingdom. Tel: (01752) 735251/
695745. Fax: (01752) 695699. Telex: 45635.

First published in 1991
Second edition (fully revised) 1995

Note: The material contained in this book is set out in good faith for general guidance and no liability can be accepted for loss or expense incurred as a result of relying in particular circumstances on statements made in the book. The laws and regulations are complex and liable to change, and readers should check the current position with the relevant authorities before making personal arrangements.

Typeset by Concept Typesetting Ltd, Salisbury, Wiltshire.
Printed and bound by The Cromwell Press Ltd, Broughton Gifford, Melksham, Wiltshire.

Contents

5

Preface
to the Second Edition

Today's governor is no silent partner in the school education team bowing quietly to the wisdom of teachers and the education authority. He or she is an active partner in the management team of the school whose collective aim is to provide the children with the best education possible.

Providing children with a worthwhile education is one of the most important things that we, as a nation, can do. It is today's children who will be tomorrow's citizens and we owe it to them to make sure that they are fully equipped for the world outside.

Why don't you become a governor? You have your unique insights and experience to bring to the job and you will be making a worthwhile contribution to the school and the community. You can influence how your school is run and the kind of education it provides. Parent governors in particular are in contact with the consumers, the children, and their representatives, other parents, and so have a vital role to play in ensuring that what the school provides is what the children need.

School governors are needed now as never before. The recent changes in education and the way schools are to be managed means that the governors of any school have real power to influence how education is delivered.

This book, now in a second fully revised and updated edition, aims to encourage everyone, particularly parents, to become a school governor. It will tell you how to become one and what to do when you are one. It gets down to basics—how can you contribute to meetings if you don't know how they work? How can you discuss reports if you don't know how to extract the relevant information from them?

I speak from experience. As governor of a primary school for nine years, three of them as vice-chairman, I progressed from a newcomer sitting nervously and silently through meeting after meeting to someone who had on occasion to chair the meeting and negotiate with officials.

I hope that any new governor reading this book will get over their shyness that much quicker and gain confidence from the practical advice I have given.

Don't be put off by people who tell you that only the headteacher and the chairman have any influence. It simply isn't true. Nor is it true that it will take up all your time, although once you get involved you may find it so interesting that you spend more and more time at it!

I have used the terms chairman and vice-chairman for consistency and because they are the official terms used in the Education Acts. Many people consider these terms sexist and other terms such as chair and chairperson may be used.

Although this book is aimed at governors in England and Wales, much of it should be useful to governors in Northern Ireland and Scotland which have their own systems.

Ideally everyone should have a turn as a school governor. If you get a chance to do so, take it. You are needed!

My thanks go to the many Chief Education Officers and their staff who took time out of their busy lives to provide me with information.

I thank Warren Comprehensive School for permission to use the advertisement from the *TES*, and Wiltshire and Waltham Forest Education Departments for permission to reproduce certain forms.

Acknowledgement is due to the Controller of Her Majesty's Stationery Office for quotes from the Education Acts of 1986 and 1988.

I thank the NCPTA for permission to reproduce its model constitution.

Many individuals have given me help and advice—forgive me for not naming you all, but please accept my thanks.

Finally, I thank my husband, Jon, who gave me his unfailing support and encouragement and survived on take-aways while this book was being written.

Polly Bird

1
Why Get Involved?

You are John or Mary Smith. You have children at the local school. You have some free time, but not a lot. Why would you want to be a school governor?

Everyone has their own answer to this question. 'I want to make sure that my child's school survives the cuts.' 'I want to help choose effective staff for the school.' 'I want to help my local community and I'm interested in education.' 'I think I can help the school manage its money better.'

Some of the reasons may seem selfish. To want to make sure that your own child does well in the education system is only natural. Being a governor won't change the attitude of your child's teacher towards him or her, but you may help to choose staff who will teach your child's class, you may vote for an amalgamation which will improve the school's organisation, or you may help to manage the money better so that savings are made for spending on computers. These things will benefit both your child and others. So what seems selfish turns into benefits for all the children in the school.

As a governor you will have a role to play in telling parents and others what the governors are doing and why. You can tell the governors what the parents want from the school, because they represent the consumers, the children.

The important thing about being a governor is not what personal reason you have for applying to do the job, but what you do to make the best use of the job when you have it.

Remember that the most important test of anything that happens in the school is whether it encourages and maintains high standards in the children's education. A governor's job is to make sure that everything the governors decide is directed towards that end.

WHAT IS A GOVERNOR?

'Governors run the school, get the front seats at school events and are more important than parents and staff.' This view of governors is still common. It is sometimes unwittingly perpetuated by schools and governors themselves. For example, I can remember the embarrassment I felt when I attended my first school event as a governor and was plucked out of the audience and told I had to sit in the front row because I was a governor. How unfair to all the other parents, and yet the headteacher had only meant to be polite.

Fortunately this sort of thing is found less often today. It gives the impression to other people that governors are privileged. It is true that in one way governors are privileged. They are privileged to be allowed to serve the school and to know what's going on, but they are not more important than everyone else.

Governors do help to run the school. Nowadays they have an increased role in the running of the school finances, choosing staff and curriculum. But the day-to-day running of the school and the way the children are taught is still the job of the headteacher and staff. Governors, headteacher and staff work together with the local education authority (LEA) to make sure that the children in the school receive the best education possible.

A governor is a manager—this used to be the more common term used—and a governor's job is to manage the school. Like any business or organisation, a school needs to have clear aims, strategies for achieving the aims and plans for the future, as well as making sure that everything runs smoothly on a day-to-day basis. The governing body of a school is a group of managers whose aim is to make sure that the school functions as it should for the benefit of the children.

What do governors do?

For a long time governors themselves were not entirely sure what their powers were. The **Education Reform Act 1988** (ERA) changed that. Guidelines and duties are clearly laid down and the governors' **Instrument and Articles of Government** clearly state what they can and cannot do.

Governors have three main roles:

● to oversee what goes on in the school—for example, what the school is doing about the curriculum. The head and staff are responsible for the day-to-day running of the school and the teaching but are accountable to the governors.

● to make decisions—for example, which staff to appoint.

● to recommend that the LEA does something—for example, repair the school building.

These are the three main jobs of a school governor. The exact nature of the duties these involve and what a governor may or may not do are set out in the Instrument and Articles of Government and these are explained in detail elsewhere (see Chapter 3).

Apart from these duties which are officially laid down, governors have other jobs to do. These jobs do not have to be done by law, but if you are going to be an effective governor they should form an important part of your role.

Talking and listening to parents
Letting parents know what governors are doing and why and finding out what parents' concerns are.

Talking and listening to staff
It is important to hear what the staff have to say about the school. This means all staff, non-teaching as well as teaching staff.

Attending school functions
To show your support for the school and to encourage the staff and children.

Attending update courses for governors
Education is changing so rapidly and is so complex that any governor should take any chance to keep up to date if he or she is to be effective.

Keeping in touch with the local community
What kind of help a school gets from the community and what reputation it has depends on how well those concerned with the school communicate with the local community.

Why should I get involved?

The question should really be, why *not* you? You have as much common sense as anyone else. You have your unique experiences and insights as an individual to bring to the school managerial situation. Someone new to the job of a governor is often a breath of fresh air and can take a view of things that LEA or staff governors who have held the office for a long time have failed to see.

The school needs you as a governor just as much as it needs the local trader or local councillor. Don't underestimate the importance of the contribution you will quickly make.

How much time?

Being a governor does take time. Being an effective governor takes more time. 'Mary Smith' turns up once a term at the regular governors meeting without having read the papers sent to her. 'John Brown' reads the information sent to him, attends the termly meetings, goes to the PTA meetings and turns up for school events as well as visiting the school regularly. It should be obvious who is going to be of more use to the school and who will get most satisfaction out of doing the job as well as possible.

The termly meetings will run for two or three hours, with possible extra meetings to complete the business. Reading the information sent before the meetings will take a couple of hours. A school visit could last from a couple of hours to a whole day. School events can last for several hours. Other meetings such as PTA meetings can take several hours.

This can seem daunting, but of course you won't be doing this all the time. It will be an evening here, a few hours there. If you are a parent governor you probably attend school events and such things as PTA meetings anyway.

Being a school governor is what you make of it. To be effective means spending time on preparation, visits and meetings, but the reward is a school that everyone can be proud of and which provides the children with the best possible education.

How long do governors serve?

Until they collapse, lapse or their term of office ends! All governors serve for four years. **The headteacher,** if choosing to be a governor, serves as long as he or she remains the headteacher.

- **Staff governors** stop being governors when they leave the school.

- **Parent governors** can remain governors for the full four years even if their children leave the school in the meantime.

- **Co-opted governors** can be dismissed by the people who co-opted them.

Some people get re-elected regularly, particularly LEA appointees, and therefore remain as governors for a great many years. Whether this is a good thing depends on how effective the person is and whether they are still active.

There are different types of schools and different types of governors.

TYPES OF SCHOOL

In England and Wales there are two types of school which are maintained by local education authorities (LEAs) from public funds ('state schools').

County schools

These schools get all of their money for buildings, staff and resources from their LEA. The LEA decides how places for children in the school are allocated.

Voluntary schools

Voluntary schools were originally set up by charities and churches. Their LEA pays for the day-to-day running costs and staff, but the schools themselves have to pay for buildings, repairs and alterations.

Voluntary schools can decide their own admissions policy but they must keep to any agreement they have made about it with the LEA.

There are three types of Voluntary school:

Controlled schools
The LEA pays all the costs for these.

Aided schools
The Voluntary body, such as a religious group, provides the building and the governors pay for outside repairs, improvements and alterations. They might get part of this back from the Department for Education (DFE). The LEA pays for the internal maintenance of the building and for the staff.

Special Agreement schools
The LEA may, by special agreement, pay from a half to three-quarters of the cost of building a new school or extending an existing one. The few special agreement schools are run by a religious body, usually Catholic.

These are not to be confused with *Special Schools*. These are set up and maintained by LEAs to provide education for children with Special Educational Needs (see Chapter 9).

Other types of school

There are now new schools which do not fit neatly into these two categories.

City Technology Colleges (CTCs) and **City Colleges for the Technology of the Arts** (CCTAs) are schools for secondary-age children with an emphasis on science and technology or technology applied to the performing or creative arts. These schools are state-aided but independent of LEAs. The capital costs are shared by the government and private sponsors. In fact, it is the government which is paying most of the bill. The DFE will pay running costs.

Grant-maintained schools have chosen to opt out of LEA control in favour of grant-maintained status. Their money comes from the Funding Agency for Schools (FAS).

Schools can be further divided into groups according to the age of the pupils they teach.

Nursery education

Nursery education is not compulsory but some authorities provide nursery classes attached to schools, or nursery schools. Nursery schools cater for children from two to five years of age, and nursery classes for children aged from three to five. The children often attend for only half a day until they are old enough to cope with the full school day. This also releases more places.

Primary education

Compulsory education starts the term after a child reaches five and is free in state maintained schools. Some authorities allow schools to take in children who are 'rising fives', that is children who are four but will be five during the term of admission. Such admissions can take place during any of the three terms where the school has room.

Primary schools usually take both boys and girls as pupils (coeducation). Pupils usually transfer to secondary education at the age of eleven in England and Wales.

The primary schools, often combined to include both age groups, are:

Infant schools
For children aged five to seven.

Junior schools
For children aged seven to eleven.

Secondary education

At the age of eleven, during the year in which they become twelve, children transfer to secondary schools. These are for children aged from eleven to sixteen years old, the age when compulsory education ends, or eighteen if the school has a sixth form. Secondary schools fall into the following categories:

Comprehensive schools
Accept pupils of all abilities.

Secondary modern schools
Give children a general education with a practical bias.

Grammar schools
Provide an academic education and have a selection procedure for admitting children.

Technical schools
Give pupils an academic and technical training.

CTCs and CCTAs
Designed to give a specialised academic and science or art technology training to able children.

Magnet schools
One LEA is considering creating magnet schools in its area. These would specialise in one area of education, such as art, music or science, and cater for pupils from fourteen to eighteen years old.

First, Middle and Upper Schools
There is another type of school system, involving first, middle and upper schools, which give a comprehensive coeducational education from five to sixteen in three stages.

In the primary education age group the children attend a first school which caters for pupils aged from five to eight, nine or ten years of age. Pupils transfer at these ages to a middle school until they are twelve, thirteen or fourteen years old and then go on to an upper school. These schools are often on the same site or close to each other to allow for continuity.

Tertiary education
Pupils who wish to do so may continue their education until the age of eighteen as a right. They can stay on in schools with their own sixth forms or they may choose to attend a separate **Sixth Form College** or **Tertiary College** if there is one in their area.

Schools with sixth forms sometimes form a **consortium** with other local schools in order to share staff and facilities and broaden the range of subjects available to their pupils.

TYPES OF GOVERNOR

All schools must have governors. There are several types:

Teacher governors

Teacher governors (staff governors) are elected in a secret ballot by the other teachers in their school. They can stay in office for four years but have to resign before the end of that time if they leave the school.

The headteacher has the right to attend any normal governors meeting but can decide whether to be a governor or not.

Parent governors

These are parents of children registered at the school, and are elected in a secret ballot by the other parents. Once in office they can stay a governor for four years, even if their child leaves the school.

Local Authority (LEA) governors

LEA governors are appointed by the local authority from recommendations by the local political parties which make up the Council. They are often known as 'political appointees'.

The authority may agree to divide the places in a certain way. This is usually done by allocating places in proportion to the size of the political parties on the Council. So the majority party would get the most places, with a lesser number going to the other parties. Nominations come from the local party political organisations.

However, some LEAs have refused to allocate any seats to minority parties, a move which has caused much bitterness among long-serving governors from the local minority parties. Whatever one's views are on this, there is no obligation on the LEAs' part to provide governors places for the minority parties.

In **Aided** or **Special Agreement** schools there must be at least one governor appointed by the LEA and, in primary schools, at least one from the minority authority such as a Parish Council, if there is one.

Although LEA governors have a political viewpoint, it is uncharitable to assume that they all follow their party line slavishly; most of them will try to put the good of the school first. Like all governors, their idea about what is the good of the school will not necessarily be yours.

On the other hand, do not assume that other types of governors have no political views. Any governor could be a member of a political party.

Foundation governors

Foundation governors are found in Voluntary schools and are appointed by the body which runs the school. They are chosen to make sure that the school is run according to its **trust deeds** and that its voluntary nature is preserved. People who want to be Foundation governors are sometimes expected to conform to certain standards, such as being regular church attenders.

Co-opted governors

These are people who are asked by the governing body to become governors of the school. Co-opted governors only remain governors for as long as the governing body decides that they should do so.

The governing bodies in LEA maintained schools are advised to co-opt governors from among those people who are not normally well represented on the governing body, such as local business people and ethnic groups. It is a good idea to co-opt a non-teaching staff member too. Although the governors do not have to follow these recommendations they will be under strong pressure to do so.

- **Sponsor governors**
  A grant-maintained school may appoint up to four sponsor governors from business who will be expected to provide financial and managerial assistance.

- **First governors**
  Governors in newly created grant-maintained schools. At least two must be parents, at least two from the local community (although one person can be both), and one from the local business community. They must outnumber the other governors.

- Figure 1 shows the different people who might attend a typical governors meeting.

Who can be a governor?

A governor must be:

- over eighteen;
- not have been sentenced to more than three months in prison;

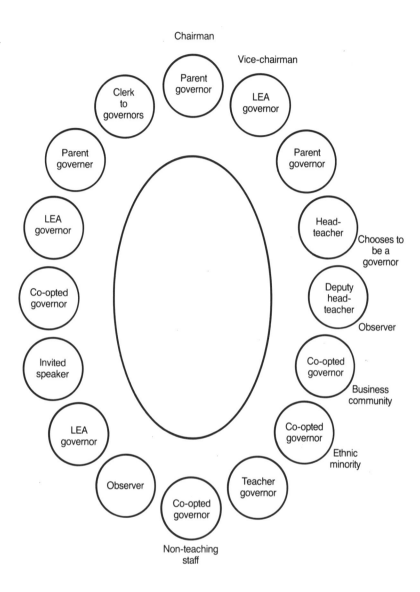

Fig. 1. People attending a typical governors' meeting of a County school of 290 pupils.

- not be bankrupt; and
- not be a member of more than four governing bodies.

Apart from the obvious restrictions stemming from the type of governor (for example, to be a parent governor you must be the parent of a child at the school), there are no other barriers to becoming a governor.

Pupils can no longer be represented on some governing bodies and so asking some older pupils to attend the meetings as observers might be a sensible idea. After all, they do represent the consumers, the pupils.

How many governors form a governing body?

The number of governors on a governing body in maintained schools varies according to the size of the school. This also decides the numbers of the various types of governor. The Education (No. 2) Act 1986 (EA 86) changed the proportions of parents to LEA governors so that LEA governors cannot make up the majority on the governing body.

The numbers and types of governor in County and Voluntary Controlled schools are most easily shown in the chart in Fig. 2.

All primary schools must have a governor from a minor authority, such as a parish council, where applicable. If an LEA decides to do so, it can treat a school of 600 or more pupils as if it is a school of a size smaller, thus reducing the numbers on the governing body.

Aided and Special Agreement schools
In these schools there must be:

- foundation governors; one must be the parent of a pupil.
- at least one parent governor;
- at least one teacher governor, two if the school contains more than 300 pupils;
- headteacher if he or she chooses to be a governor;
- at least one governor appointed by the LEA;
- in a primary school, at least one governor from a minor authority, such as a parish council, where applicable.

Foundation governors in Aided and Special Agreement schools must outnumber the other governors by two in governing bodies of less

Composition of governing bodies

County and Voluntary Controlled schools

Up to 99 pupils
2 parents
2 LEA appointees
1 teacher
3 co-opted (or 1 co-opted and 2 Foundation at Controlled schools)
1 headteacher (if head chooses)

100–299 pupils
3 parents
3 LEA appointees
1 teacher
4 co-opted (or 1 co-opted and 3 Foundation at Controlled schools)
1 headteacher (if head chooses)

300–599 pupils
4 parents
4 LEA appointees
2 teachers
5 co-opted (or 1 co-opted and 4 Foundation at Controlled schools)
1 headteacher (if head chooses)

600 or more pupils
5 parents
5 LEA appointees
2 teachers
6 co-opted (or 2 co-opted and 4 Foundation at Controlled schools)
1 headteacher (if head chooses)

Fig. 2. Numbers and types of governor.

than eighteen people, or by three in larger bodies. Apart from that there is no restriction on the size of governing bodies in these kinds of schools.

Grant-maintained schools have 3–5 parent governors (primary) or 5 (secondary). The governing body must include first governors who must outnumber the other governors. There are 1 or 2 teacher governors as specified with the headteacher ex-officio. There can be up to four sponsor governors and the Secretary of State may appoint up to two extra governors.

CHECKLIST

1. You can be a governor—you have a unique contribution to make.

2. Don't be put off by the amount of time needed to be effective—you don't do it all at once.

3. Find out what type of school you will be a governor of.

4. Decide what kind of governor you want to be, for example, a parent governor or an LEA governor. You might find one route easier than another.

'No wonder they're having to advertise for governors!'

2
First Steps—How To Become a Parent Governor

Many people ask 'How do I become a school governor?' as if becoming a governor was something that only special people could do. They think that the title of 'governor' sets people apart and that it is not a job for 'ordinary' people. Others are put off by the official procedures involved. Filling in forms and making speeches seem complicated.

In the previous chapter I have mentioned how teacher governors, co-opted governors or local authority (LEA) governors are chosen. However, because of the increase in the number of parent governors, most people will get to the governing body by this route.

There has to be a particular way of choosing parent governors which is fair to everyone. It is not really complicated. This chapter will explain how to become a parent governor.

Some parents will have taken part in elections in other places and so be used to it. For those who haven't this is how it works:

Steps to becoming a governor
1. Wait for a vacancy to occur.
2. Become nominated.
3. Attend an election meeting.
4. Vote.
5. Get elected.
6. Accept the post.

WAITING FOR A VACANCY

Vacancies usually occur in September at the beginning of the school year when parent governors have left or resigned. Now that parent governors can stay in the job for four years even when their child has left the school, vacancies may occur less often. So be patient!

Vacancies can occur at other times during the school year if a parent governor dies, resigns, or loses his office by failing to attend any meeting for twelve months.

Your LEA has a duty to make sure that every parent or guardian of a child in a school is told about any vacancy and forthcoming election for a parent governor. (Parent in this book is taken to include legal guardian.) Parents are informed by post or by sending a letter home with the child ('pupil post').

The local education authority (LEA) makes the overall decisions about how the elections are run, but the schools are left to work out the details of organisation. LEAs offer guidance about how the elections should be conducted in order to ensure fairness and coherence throughout their authorities.

BEING NOMINATED

Although there is no guarantee that you will be elected if you stand as a governor, you cannot be considered unless you are nominated. The more people who stand for any governor's job, the more choice the parents will have.

Every parent will be sent a nomination form. Authorities usually want a candidate to have one or two **seconders**, that is people who support your nomination. In that case, their names, addresses and signatures must also appear on the form. (See Fig. 3.)

You can wait for someone to ask you if you want to be nominated, but there is nothing to stop you deciding to stand yourself and asking other parents to be seconders. In fact, this is how most nominations are made. So do not feel shy about putting yourself forward. In schools where there is a shortage of willing parents, the school will be only too pleased that someone is interested.

GETTING ELECTED

Will there be an election?

If only one person is nominated for a vacancy, the governors can decide to accept that person as a governor without an election.

If there are no candidates, the governing body can co-opt a parent who has a child at the school. If this is not possible, it can co-opt the parent of a school-age child who is not at the school.

Where there are two or more candidates for a parent governor vacancy, an election must be held.

Election meeting

The LEA is responsible for making sure that the election is carried out by secret ballot and that parents are informed by post or 'pupil post'. Names of all the candidates should be sent to all the parents

Form PC/PG/2

_____SCHOOL

ELECTION OF PARENT GOVERNOR - NOMINATION FORM

NOMINEE: I, (names in full)_____

_____of (address)_____

_____ Post Code_____,
would be prepared to stand as a candidate in the election for Parent
Governor(s) to serve on the Governing Body of the above named school.

I am a parent/guardian of the following pupil(s) who are registered at the
school:-

| Name(s) | Date of Birth | Class/Form/Tutor Group |

S P E C I M E N

Signed:_____   Date:_____
_____

PROPOSED BY: (full name)_____

Address:_____

Parent/Guardian: (name/s of pupil/s)_____

          Class/form/tutor group:_____

          Signed:_____   Date:_____
_____

SECONDED BY: (full name)_____

Address:_____

Parent/Guardian: (name/s of pupil/s) _____

          Class/form/tutor group:_____

Signed: _____   Date:_____
_____

This form should be returned to the Clerk to the Governing Body,
c/o the_____School
by_____(Date).

0389A

Fig. 3. Model nomination form
(Reproduced with permission of Wiltshire Education Department.)

with details of any meetings at the school at which the parents can meet the candidates.

Although ideally it is better to hold more than one election meeting to allow parents who work or who have child-care problems to attend, only one meeting is usually held. It is often held at the same time as another school event in order to attract as many parents as possible into the school.

Some schools find that a lot of parents attend such meetings, others that parents do not respond well whatever is provided. The important thing is that the school must try.

You should try to attend these meetings if you wish to become a governor. Even if only a few parents attend, other parents will learn by word of mouth about the candidates who were there and what they said. In addition, the parents who turn out for the meetings are the ones most likely to vote!

Speeches

Candidates are usually asked to say a few words at the election meeting. This is to give the other parents a chance to get to know you. It is also the time when you can try to convince people that you would make a good governor.

Speeches terrify many prospective governors (and even experienced governors, I might add). All that is usually required in this case is a short statement in which you give your name and a few details about yourself, and say why you want to be a governor of the school and what you could do for the school.

- If you are nervous, write your statement down and read it out. You are not aiming to become Prime Minister, simply to let other parents know a bit about you.

- Do stand up to say your piece so that parents can see you and so that your voice carries more.

- Wait for chattering to die down before you speak.

- If you are required to answer questions, do so as honestly and simply as possible.

Remember, the audience wants to hear what you have to say. Details you might include are:

- name;
- number of children at the school;
- how long you have been connected with the school;
- any relevant experience of the school;
- other relevant experience;
- why you want to be a governor.

Don't forget to mention if you have had an older child who has been through the school. Include the length of time from your eldest child, even if she or he has now left. You might want to mention such things as bringing your youngest child to the school Toddlers Club every week or the fact that you go on school trips with your child's class.

If you work at a youth club, are from an under-represented ethnic group, or are active in the local community, these are things which might be relevant.

When you are telling everyone why you want to be a school governor you might say that you:

- want to help improve the quality of education for all the children in the school;

Susan Black. Mother of Charlie (3R), Anne (1C) and Tim (2 years). I have been bringing my children to the school for four years since Charlie was in the school Toddlers Club. Now I take Tim to the Toddlers Club every week and I also go on class outings with 3R and 1C.

I help at the After School Club at St Mary's Church on three evenings a week.

I would like to be a governor because I think more women should be on the committee. I want to help to improve the quality of education for all the children in the school. I especially want to encourage more contact between the parents, governors and staff so that we can exchange ideas and work together for the good of the school.

If elected, I would be an active governor and would make myself available to talk to parents as often as possible.

Fig. 4. Model Statement

- want to improve home/school liaison;

- want to make the governing body more representative by increasing the number of women or governors of ethnic origin;

- want to make sure that the money is properly spent for the benefit of the school;

- want to take part in staff selection in order to ensure that the school gets the best staff available.

Statement for ballot box

In some schools it is the custom to ask candidates to provide a short written statement to go over the ballot box as a reminder to the parents who attended the meeting and for the information of those who didn't. Sometimes you will be asked for a photograph of yourself as well.

Write a short statement including the items suggested for your speech (see Fig. 4). Write it clearly or type it. The photograph can simply be one out of a booth or your family album. No need for specially taken portraits!

VOTING

All parents will receive details about the candidates, and when and where the voting will take place. They will also be told about how to vote by post if they need to do so. A model voting slip is illustrated in Fig. 5.

Someone is chosen to make sure that the voting takes place in a fair manner and to oversee the counting of the votes (the **returning officer**). This person should be unconnected with the school, if possible.

It is better if staff do not take part in looking after the ballot box or counting votes because they are so closely involved with the school. And they are needed in the classrooms!

Suitable people might be found among the business community or the police who would be willing to undertake the task.

The **ballot box** will usually be in the school for a full day—if possible from about 8.30 a.m to 8.30 p.m to allow as many parents as possible to come into the school to vote. There should be someone available to watch the box at all times and to check parents' names off a list so that no cheating occurs.

ELECTION OF PARENT GOVERNOR

_____ SCHOOL

There are two vacancies to be filled and you should vote for not more than two candidates. Please indicate your choice by placing an 'X' in the box opposite the name(s) of the candidate(s) you wish to support.

I Name of Candidate

I ....

I Name of Candidate

I ....

I Name of Candidate

I ....

I Name of Candidate

I ....

SPECIMEN

Please return this voting paper to the Clerk to the Governors,

c/o _____ School, in the

envelope provided to arrive at the school not later

than _____ (Date).

0389A

Fig. 5. Model voting slip
(Reproduced with permission of Wiltshire Education Department.)

Postal ballots should be received by the school before the end of the voting day. They are added unopened to the box and are then opened in front of witnesses when the votes are counted.

Do go and vote yourself. And do not be shy about voting for yourself. All the other candidates will be voting for themselves!

THE RESULT

Candidates are invited to be present when the votes are counted to ensure fair play and to get the news first. In any case, the returning officer should keep a record of the count and ensure that all parents are notified of the result the next day by pupil post.

The new parent governors will be the candidates who get the most votes.

The ballot papers and records should be kept by the headteacher for at least six months in case there are any arguments later on.

ACCEPTANCE

Once your name has been declared the winner of the ballot, you are a governor and you do not need to wait for the LEA to confirm this. However, the LEA will normally write to you to confirm your appointment and welcome you to the governing body (see Figs. 6 and 7).

The LEA will also ask you to provide your address and telephone number for circulation so that you can be contacted by parents or anyone else with a reasonable reason to do so.

All parents will be informed in writing of the result of the election.

You have now done everything necessary to become a school parent governor. Well done! The following chapters will tell you how to go about your job in the most effective way.

CHECKLIST

1. Wait for a vacancy to occur.
2. Ask someone to nominate you.
3. Attend election meeting.
4. Write statement for ballot box.
5. Vote.
6. Attend the count.
7. Accept position.

London Borough of Waltham Forest,
Martin Shepherd, MA., M.Sc.,
Chief Education Officer,
Municipal Offices, High Road, Leyton, London E10 5QJ
01-527 5544

WALTHAM FOREST

Fax No only 527 5544 ext 5163

Malcolm Meredith, B.A.
Deputy Chief Education Officer and Senior Education Officer (Schools):
George Chetham, B.A.
Senior Education Officer (Finance, Administration and Development):
Evelyn Carpenter, B.A.
Senior Education Officer (Community and Further Education)

Dear . . . .
. . . . .School Governing Body
Welcome to the Governing Body of . . . . School. I hope that you enjoy your association with your School.
With this letter you will find a package of papers containing the Instrument and Articles of Government. These are the legal guidelines on how to carry out your duties. Also in the package are copies of other documents which your colleague-Governors have received recently and which I hope will help you in your work as a Governor. When you attend your first meeting, you can collect from the School a Governors' Handbook binder, for these papers. Keep the handbook in a safe place—during your term of office you will probably have to refer to it many times and will get other papers which you may wish to put inside it. You may collect, at the same time, a copy of the DES Guide to the Law, which explains the Regulations relating to school governance.
The Governing Bodies Unit, a part of the Education Department, is there to help you to be an effective Governor. The people in the Unit are Pat Barford, who is the Assistant Education Officer responsible for Governing Bodies, and Carol Deer and Susan Gill, the administrative staff.
Regular training sessions are provided for Governors and we will let you know about them in good time and invite you to attend.
We must ensure that you receive all your papers for meetings and other documents, so it is very important that our records about you are correct. Please check the address we have used on this letter. Have we got it right, including your (very important) post code? If you move house or if your telephone number at home or at work changes, please let the Unit know as soon as possible so that we can keep in touch with you.
There is a part of the acceptance form, which is attached to this letter, where we ask you to let us have some personal details. Please fill this in and return it, to help us to tailor the service we provide to the needs of our Governors.
The information you give us about yourself will be stored on a computer and will be available only to authorised staff of the Education Department. Your fellow-Governors and the School which you govern will be given only your name, address and contact telephone number(s). We will not release your personal information to anyone else without your permission.
Your appointment as a Governor will take immediate effect and you will cease to be a Governor on 31st August 1993. You may, of course, resign at any time, if you wish or need to!
You will be advised of the date of the next Governing Body meeting.
I wish you a happy and interesting term of office.
Yours sincerely,

J.M. Shepherd
Clerk to the Governors

Fig. 6. Acceptance Letter
(Reproduced with permission of Waltham Forest Education Department.)

APPOINTMENT OF   GOVERNOR

To: The Chief Education Officer   From:
      London Borough of Waltham Forest
      Municipal Offices
      High Road Leyton
      London E10 5QJ

I have read and understood the disqualifications listed overleaf.

I accept appointment as a Governor of

as set out in your letter dated

My daytime telephone number is ....

My home telephone number is ....(if different from above)

The following information will be confidential and is intended to help in
the drawing up of anonymous statistics.

I would describe myself as being of the following ethnic origin: (please tick)

European: U.K.   [ ]   Asian: Bangladeshi   [ ]

            Irish Republic [ ]   East African   [ ]

            Greek   [ ]   Indian   [ ]

            Turkish   [ ]   Pakistani   [ ]

Other European origin   Other Asian origin   [ ]
including Old Commonwealth
and U.S.A.   [ ] .   Other. If you do not see yourself
                                           as part of any of these groups,
Caribbean   [ ]   please specify

African   [ ]   ....

I would describe myself as disabled [ ] please tick if appropriate

If you have ticked this box, please let us know how you would describe your

disability..

Signed: .... Date: ....

For disqualifications to holding the office of governor, please see overleaf

SB/M5/CMD
Governing Bodies Section

Fig. 7. Appointment form. (Reproduced with permission of Waltham Forest Education Department.)

3
Help! I'm a Governor—What
Do I Do Now?

Now that you are a governor you need to prepare yourself for the job. You cannot be effective unless you know something about your school and have met the staff and parents. You will also need to obtain some general information about the governors' role.

USEFUL INFORMATION

LEA sources
Together with a letter of welcome, your LEA must send you copies of the **Instrument and Articles of Government** for your school.

The Instrument tells you about the constitution of the governing body, that is, how many governors there will be and who they can be. It also provides the rules for running meetings and explains such things as how many people are needed before resolutions can be passed (the **quorum**), how the chairman should be elected, rules for attendance, and so on.

The Articles of Government tell governors what they may or may not do, and, together with the Instrument, are legal documents.
   The Articles of Government explain the governors' duties concerning:

- the curriculum;
- sex education;
- terms, sessions and holidays;
- discipline;
- exclusion of pupils;
- finance;
- Annual Report to Parents;
- Annual Parents Meeting;
- admissions;

32

- appointment and dismissal of staff;
- school premises.

The LEA will usually provide an explanatory leaflet or book about the Instrument and Articles because the legal language is difficult to understand. Read all these papers carefully. They provide the basis for how you conduct yourself as a governor.

Your LEA might also send you the Department for Education (DFE) publication *School Governors: A Guide to the Law.* This is a loose-leaf file containing information for governors about their legal responsibilities. It is designed to have extra chapters added when new topics arise. This is a clear and readable guide and if your LEA does not send you one, ask the clerk to the governors if he or she can get one for you.

Some LEAs content themselves with sending new governors the Instrument and Articles of Government and the DFE guide. Most LEAs, however, go to great trouble to provide a lot of **background information** for new governors. Such information could include:

- information about LEA governor support unit;
- advice for new governors;
- information about where new governors can go for help;
- LEA newsletter to governors;
- LEA policy documents on topics such as the curriculum, equal opportunities or community education;
- National Association of Governors and Managers (NAGM) information and papers;
- information about associations for parent governors;
- details of governor training;
- LEA school governors' handbook;
- information particularly for parent governors;
- secondary school admissions policy;
- suggested reading list;
- addresses of resource centres;
- description of how the LEA works.

Of course, not all LEAs will provide all of this information. If you decide that you could benefit from some of the information listed but your LEA hasn't sent it to you, again the clerk is the person to approach. The headteacher or the chairman of the governors might have one or two booklets for you to borrow. You could also ask for the address of your nearest education resource centre and find out what information is available there for governors.

Books

Other helpful books (besides this one!) are listed in the Further Reading section at the end of this book. If your LEA hasn't sent you a recommended reading list ask at your local library or education resource centre.

Your local authority will also have a booklet giving general information about the LEA which you should get hold of and read.

Training

Your LEA is now obliged to provide training for governors, but how this is done is left to the individual LEAs. If there is a local training course offered you will be well advised to sign up for it as soon as possible. It is likely to cover such topics as finance, the curriculum and racism. (More information about training is given in Chapter 12.)

School prospectus

Since 1980 all schools have been obliged to issue a prospectus for parents and other interested people giving information about the school. Ask for a copy when you telephone the school to arrange your first visit. It will give you some background about the school's aims and practice (see Fig. 8).

The **minimum information** which should be in the prospectus is:

- name, address and telephone number of school;

- names of headteacher and chairman of the governors:

- type of school (*eg* middle, special, primary);

- details of arrangements for visits by prospective parents;

- details of school curriculum for different age groups;

- if and how sex education is taught;

- careers education and guidance (secondary schools);

- school's religious affiliation, if any;

- details of RE teaching and arrangements made for withdrawing children if parents wish;

- provision for children with Special Education Needs;

- how the education in school is organised (*eg* setting, integrated);

- homework requirements;

- arrangements for pastoral care;

- policy on discipline;

- school rules;

- school societies and other activities;

- school clothing policy and cost of uniform if needed;

- Welsh language policy (in Wales);

- policy for entering children in public exams;

- exam results;

- changes to be made after the prospectus has been published;

School aims

This school aims to promote the full potential of each pupil in all aspects of learning: intellectual, practical, creative, aesthetic, moral, social and personal.

This school aims to ensure that each pupil receives the necessary help and equal opportunities to achieve that full potential. Each pupil will be encouraged to achieve his or her highest academic standards and practical and creative skills.

Pupils will be encouraged to take responsibility for their own behaviour and to become highly motivated and adaptable. They will be encouraged both to work independently and to co-operate with others.

We aim to ensure that each pupil develops as a flexible, sensitive, caring individual fully equipped to take his or her place in our changing and multicultural society.

Fig. 8. Statement of aims from a school prospectus.

- year to which prospectus refers with a disclaimer about possible changes;

- details of the possibility of publishing the prospectus in Welsh or any other language (remembering that it is to be available free of charge).

Most schools will want their prospectuses to contain much more than this, particularly now that the delegation of financial control to schools means that they will want to attract more pupils to get more money.

When you read the prospectus and later, when you visit the school, note what **extras** are available. For example, is there:

- a separate Nursery class?
- before or after school care?
- a Youth Club after school?
- a parents and toddlers club?
- a Parent/Staff Association?

You are likely to find that much of the information included in the Annual Report to Parents will also be included in the prospectus.

You can see from the items listed above that you can obtain a lot of information about the school by careful reading of the school prospectus. It should give you ideas about what to look out for on your first visit and suggest possible questions when you meet the headteacher and staff.

YOUR FIRST SCHOOL VISIT

All governors should visit the school, ideally on a regular basis. The first visit is particularly important because it will give you an **immediate impression** of how other people see the school. (Is the atmosphere welcoming? Are the buildings in good repair? Is the decoration cheerful and in good condition? Is the children's work displayed?)

Even if you are a parent governor, you might not have seen all of the school, nor seen a class in action, so do not assume that you know the school well enough to miss making a visit. (Have you seen the staffroom, toilets, library, annex, outbuildings, catering facilities, gymnasium, labs?)

Remember, though, that you have no right to visit the school. You can only do so under any arrangements made by the governing body with the headteacher. If the headteacher tells you that you are welcome to call in at any time, it is a **privilege**, not a right.

Making arrangements to visit

Don't just turn up at the school and expect to be shown round or be allowed to wander round on your own. The school is a working environment and your visit must fit in with the routines of the school and the needs of the children.

There is a **safety** aspect as well. Schools are vulnerable to intruders and you should always make your presence known to the secretary. You wouldn't want other people to wander round without letting anyone know and possibly causing damage to the school or harm to the children, and so you must make sure that your own visit is known.

- Telephone the school first. You will probably get the school secretary who can then phone you back with details of the arrangements to visit, or the headteacher might wish to contact you personally.

- Do not demand a visit, ask. You do not want to antagonise the headteacher before you've even seen round the school!

- Don't forget to ask for a copy of the school prospectus.

- Do try to go on the date and at the time suggested. Headteachers have full timetables and will have had to make special arrangements to see you. Classes may be out on visits, or there may be a special assembly to arrange so your visit must fit in with any timetabling or problems.

Preparation

Having made your arrangements to visit you can do some preparation by reading the school prospectus and preparing a few questions for the headteacher. (What sort of problems have the staff had in preparing for the National Curriculum? What arrangements does the school make to ensure that the teachers and pupils in the Annex are secure and have contact with the school? Does this school have a special relationship with any of the local secondary schools? Do local businesses give talks to help careers information?)

You might also want to ask a few practical questions about your job as a governor. (What arrangements does the school like governors to make about visits? Do governors automatically get informed about and invited to school events? Would it be possible to meet some of the staff informally, perhaps one lunchtime or break?)

On a practical note, it is common in many schools now for staff to be addressed by their **first name** by pupils and colleagues. However, it is still considered impolite for a newcomer, such as a new governor, to address an adult by their first name unless asked to do so. So even if the name on the school sign says 'Headteacher—Annie Brown', don't march in and say 'Hi, Annie!' 'Hello, Ms Brown' is still the correct approach.

Do not smoke in school. Apart from the safety aspect, you will give a bad impression to both pupils and staff. Whatever staff may do about smoking in private, they will not want you to smoke in front of the children.

What you will see

What you actually get shown on your first visit will be entirely up to the headteacher who will either show you round personally or have instructed a colleague to do so. Inevitably this means that some places you expected to see may get missed out. If you think that you should see a particular place, do ask politely. However, there may be a perfectly good reason why you will have to wait until another time, for example, if a lab is closed for safety reasons, building work is going on in the annex or exams are taking place in the gymnasium.

Places you can expect to see include:

- classrooms;
- hall/s;
- staffroom;
- toilets;
- library;
- laboratories;
- art room;
- music room;
- craft, design and technology (CDT) workshop;
- gymnasium;
- playground/s;
- annex;
- outbuildings;
- resources room;
- kitchen/catering facilities;
- home economics room;

- headteacher's room;
- secretary's room;
- medical room.

Do ask to see the **boys' toilets** (not everybody's favourite room!) They seem to be a guide as to how well the maintenance of the school is being managed. They are also an indication, of course, about how boys treat their facilities!

Make a note of anything which you hoped to see but weren't shown so that you can ask to see them on a subsequent visit.

You will probably be shown some **classrooms,** possibly one or two in use, but don't expect to be allowed to go in and have a long chat with any teacher busy teaching. If you are allowed in you will be briefly introduced. If you are allowed to stay while the class is in session you must be careful not to disturb the class too much.

Visiting a primary class is often easier than in a secondary school because the work is done in a more informal way. There will probably be groups of children working around the class and you might be able to look at the room and have a few words with some of them while the teacher is helping other groups. In a secondary school where classwork is more formal you may not be able to do much more than say hello to the teacher and have a brief look round the walls.

In both cases it will benefit you more to arrange another visit to meet some of the staff informally and perhaps get permission to sit in on a class, always remembering, of course, that you are there only by permission and are not there to judge teaching performance.

What to look for

How can you tell what a school is like just by walking around it? The answer is, of course, that you can't, but you can tell a lot about a school from what you observe on a visit, even a brief one.

Ask yourself the following questions:

- How do the children move about the school? Is it in an orderly fashion or do they run along shouting?

- How much of the children's work is displayed and where?

- Are signs and notices displayed in languages other than English?

- Is the atmosphere as you enter the school welcoming?

- Is it made clear to visitors where to go?

- Are the toilets inside or outside the school? Are they in good condition? In secondary schools do the girls' toilets have sanitary towel or tampon dispensers?

- Is the playground bare or have efforts been made to provide greenery? Is any grass area nicely kept?

- Are there outside sports facilities?

- Do the children work in groups or are they seated in formal rows?

- What kind of desks do the children sit at? New or old-fashioned?

- How difficult is it to go from one floor to another, or from the annex to the main school building?

- How large is the library? Is it carpeted and welcoming?

- Where are the fire escapes? Are the fire doors blocked?

- How many halls are there? Is there a stage? What are the halls used for?

You will not notice all these as you walk round on the first visit, but the list should give you an idea of the sort of things to notice. For example, you might wonder why a school had no work by children on the walls and the children were expected to sit in uniform rows to learn. Is this an ideal atmosphere for learning? Would your child feel welcome here?

Visiting a class

If you are given the chance to visit a class while teaching is in progress, you must be careful to disrupt it as little as possible.

You will probably be given a brief introduction to the teacher who may then invite you to spend a few minutes looking around and talking to the pupils.

Do not abuse such an opportunity. The teacher is in charge of the class and cannot take time off there and then to have a long conversation with you. You will no doubt want to arrange to meet some of the staff on another occasion and can have your talk then.

What should you look for?

Have a look around the room, which you can do while the class goes on working. Note the kind of work on the wall and what sort of books and equipment are on display. There is more likely to be a greater amount of **display material** in a primary school because in secondary schools pupils do not necessarily stay in their own class-rooms for all their lessons. In their case you would want to spend more time looking around laboratories, art rooms and libraries.

In a primary classroom you could look out for such things as a good range of books on display, and different areas for various activities such as sand play, water play, woodwork and science. In a secondary school you could look out for work on the wall, the age of the books and equipment, and whether pupils have to share them.

Contact with the children

Have a look at the work the children are doing. If you are allowed to talk to them, always ask before looking at their work. Good manners should not desert you just because children are involved. Remember that some children might feel shy about showing a stranger their work.

With small children, get down to their level. It is offputting for them to have to keep looking up to talk to an adult. Ask questions like: 'Would you tell me about what you are doing, please? It looks very interesting.' 'What other things do you like to do in class?' 'Can you show me your favourite piece of work?'

Older children could explain to you how the computer works or what their chemistry experiment is about.

Don't talk about your own child

Parent governors must be careful not to engage in a long talk about their own child. It is very tempting for both teacher and governor to start a discussion about the governor's child because it is something they both have in common, but a governor's visit is not the time or the place to do that. You might well have become a governor because you wanted to improve your child's education, but your responsibility is now to the education of all the children. If the teacher does start a conversation about your child, politely deflect it by saying: 'It's nice to hear how Johnny is doing, but may I talk you to about that later, please? Could you tell me something about how the class is coping with the new curriculum subject/new reading scheme/lack of books?'

Make sure that you yourself don't raise the subject of your individual child on a visit, otherwise everyone will think that you do not have the interests of the whole school at heart.

Talking to staff

Try to arrange to meet the staff at a lunchtime or break so that you can have an informal chat with them about the school and any problems they are facing. You might learn, for example, that there is a shortage of computer equipment or that there is a general problem with discipline. These are the kinds of things that you would not necessarily discover from your visit.

Make the effort to learn the **names** of the staff and what particular **positions** they hold, if any: for example, Mr Grey, Head of Geography or Miss Jane, special responsibility for language development. This will give you an idea of the sort of questions it would be useful to ask individual teachers.

If you have particular questions which you want to put to the headteacher, arrange to have a talk with him or her on a separate occasion when he or she can take time to discuss the school with you at more length.

After the visit

Before you leave the building go and thank the headteacher or leave a message of **thanks** with the secretary. This is a courtesy and also lets the secretary know that you have left the building.

As soon after the visit as possible, make some **notes** about what you have seen and heard. This is useful, not only as a reminder to yourself about what you have observed, but also as a basis for a report to the governing body.

Record your impressions of the building, the atmosphere, discipline, problems, areas of excellence, and anything else which seems to you to be useful.

Report to the governors

In many schools the item 'Governors' report' is permanently on the agenda. The aim is to remind governors who have visited the school to share their impressions with the rest of the governing body. This is particularly important in schools where visits are made on a rota basis and so many governors will not have made a recent visit to the school.

The report need not be long and can be written and passed round at the meeting. Even if the item is not on the agenda it is sensible to share your discoveries with the others in order that any problems can be discussed. (See Fig. 9.)

Subsequent visits

Once you have made the first visit, subsequent visits will be easier.

**Report to the governors of a school visit made
on March 15th by Mary Smith**

This was my first visit to the school and I was shown round by Mr Markham, the deputy head. I was shown all the building except the library which was closed for reorganisation.

I was able to visit one class in each year, except the fifth. The fifth year were unavailable because they were sitting their mock GCSE exams.

I was impressed by the calm, working atmosphere of the school and the obvious enthusiasm of the staff and pupils. Pupils' work was much in evidence and showed high standards, particularly in art.

The school has very good facilities. I was particularly impressed by the separate dance room with the special flooring. The premises are generally in good condition and it was a pleasure to walk round a school undecorated by graffiti. There is a problem with litter but the school is just about to launch an anti-litter campaign and I will report on its effect after my next visit.

I understand there is a problem with lunchtime supervision and so I will be making a special visit next half-term to sample the food and look at the supervision. Again, I will report back on this.

I would like to thank the staff and pupils for making me feel welcome and look forward to my next visit.

Fig. 9. Model governor's report after a school visit.

You will know the school buildings and the staff and know what you are permitted to do on a visit.

After this first general visit you may wish to make a special visit in order to concentrate on a particular aspect of school provision. For example, you may ask to stay for a school dinner and take an interest in the quality of food and lunchtime supervision, and visit the kitchens.

- Visiting the school is the only way to have some understanding of what the pupils and staff are experiencing. An efficient governor will take every opportunity to see for him or herself how the school operates.

CHECKLIST

1. Telephone to arrange a visit.

2. Ask for a copy of the school prospectus.

3. Read the prospectus and any other useful literature.

4. Prepare some questions for the headteacher.

5. Visit on the date and time suggested.

6. Be polite in addressing pupils and staff.

7. Do not smoke.

8. Observe but do not disrupt.

9. Arrange to talk to staff informally on another occasion.

10. Do not have a lengthy discussion about your own child.

11. Thank the headteacher.

12. Make notes soon after your visit and use them to prepare a short report to the governors.

4
Preparing For Meetings

Meetings can seem to have a logic of their own to an outsider. How does anyone know what is going on and what should happen next?

This chapter and the next will take the mystery out of meetings. They will tell how meetings are organised, what happens in them, and how you can contribute to them successfully. You might even end up enjoying them!

TERMLY GOVERNORS MEETING

The governors must meet at least once each term. These regular termly meetings are one of the most important parts of a governor's job.

Why are governors meetings held?

Meetings are occasions where people exchange information and ideas, and take decisions. As a governor, you will learn what is going on in the school, what the staff are worried about, what the LEA and government requirements are, what problems are current in the school, and so on.

There will also be decisions to be taken: 'Shall we call in the architect to explain why the repairs to the toilets are still unsatisfactory?' 'Who will be on the subcommittee to help draft the report to the parents?'

Where and when do they take place?

The meetings take place on the school premises during the school day or the evening. Most schools try to arrange them out of school hours. The time will obviously not suit all governors, but as plenty of notice is given you should try to make arrangements to attend.

Child-care arrangements

If you have children of pre-school age and need to attend a daytime governors meeting, try asking the headteacher whether they can sit in a classroom or staffroom with a helper for a couple of hours. If evening meetings are a problem for parents then the governors should consider holding a **crèche**. Some LEAs would look favourably on a request for help in funding such a crèche.

Seats and desks

It is usual to sit in a hall or class or staffroom in a circle/square behind desks. Everyone can then see and talk to each other and you can rest your paper (and cups of coffee) and make notes. It also gives people a sense of security to have a desk to sit behind.

If there are no desks or if the chairman and the clerk are the only ones to have a desk, why not mention the point. Other governors have probably been dying to have somewhere to put their papers, but are afraid to ask.

OTHER MEETINGS

Often there will be extra meetings to attend. Other meetings you might be asked to attend are:

- staff appointments (see Chapter 7);

- subcommittees—governors delegated to discuss items and report back to the main meeting;

- exclusion meetings—to decide whether a pupil should be excluded from school;

- Parent Staff Association (PSA) meetings;

- meeting to present the Annual Report to the parents;

- action group meetings—meetings of interest groups.

Not all governors will want or feel able to attend all these meetings. Bear in mind, however, that the more of these extra meetings that you attend, the more you will get to know parents, staff and pupils, and the more you will learn about what is going on in the school. The governor who only attends the main meeting is not getting a rounded picture of school life and remains largely unknown to parents and staff alike. The more visible and available you make yourself, the more people will be inclined to express their opinions and concerns about the school to you.

HOW LONG ARE GOVERNORS MEETINGS?

The main governors meetings usually last from two to three hours depending on the amount of business to get through, the length of time the clerk to the governors can be available, the rule concerning the letting of individual school premises, when the caretaker has to get home, and, of course, the stamina of the governors.

ATTENDANCE

You must turn up for at least one meeting a year in order to remain a governor. Some governors do attend only the one meeting a year required. They arrive, argue about decisions previously made by the governing body and then are not seen again until the following year.

You, of course, will not be so irresponsible and selfish. You should attend each term's meeting in order to keep an overall view of what is going on and to make informed decisions.

If you cannot get to a meeting, write to or telephone the clerk or the chairman of the governors explaining your absence and sending your **apologies**. This is not only courteous but practical. Without your apology the start of the meeting might be delayed while everyone waits for you. Try not to miss a meeting too often.

INFORMATION FOR THE MEETING

At least seven days before your first meeting you will be sent:

- minutes of the previous meeting;
- agenda;
- reports relevant to items on the agenda;
- other items of interest to the governing body.

Try to read the information sent to you before your first meeting. If you have not received a copy of the school prospectus ask the school secretary for one.

Minutes of the previous meeting

These are a record of who attended the meeting, the main points of discussion, what resolutions were put forward and what decisions were taken. After making any amendments asked for by the governors, the chair will sign them as an accurate record of the meeting.

The minutes of each meeting must be put on display in the school.

J.M. Grey
Clerk to the Governors
County Hall
Moonshire M11

21 October 1994   Tel: Moonshire 1234

Dear Governor,

A meeting of the Governing Body of Downtown Primary School will take place on 4th November 1994 at 7.30 p.m. at the school.

Yours faithfully

J.M. Grey
Clerk to the Governors

Agenda

1. Apologies for absence.
2. Welcome to new members.
3. Election of Chairman.
4. Election of Vice-chairman.
5. Minutes of the meeting held on 13 June 1994.
6. Matters arising from the minutes.
7. Headteacher's report (enclosed).
8. Financial report (enclosed).
9. Discussion of admissions policy.
10. Speaker—Mrs Thomas, Schools Catering Manager.
11. Governors' reports.
12. Prizes.

Confidential business:

13. Staff appointments.
14. Exclusion of pupils.
15. Accidents to pupils.

16. Any other business.
17. Date and time of next meeting.

Fig. 10. Model agenda

Agenda

Before every meeting you will sent an agenda which will set out the order of business for the meeting. LEAs usually send out a standard agenda, but this will vary between authorities. (See Fig. 10).

You will usually expect to find on it:

- apologies for absence;
- minutes of the last meeting;
- matters arising from the minutes;
- LEA reports;
- other reports;
- financial report;
- reports from governors;
- headteacher's report;
- staff appointments;
- prizes;
- confidential business, which might include:
  —exclusions;
  —accidents to pupils;
- any other business;
- date and time of next meeting.

You might also find:

- welcome to new members;
- subcommittee reports;
- notices;
- invited speaker.

Governors can add items to the agenda for discussion by contacting the clerk before the agenda gets sent out.

Any three governors can call an extra meeting if they want to discuss something urgently or they consider a subject needs more discussion than the meeting could give.

The chairman will make sure that every item on the agenda is discussed in turn.

Matters arising

The clerk should give you a report about the result of any decisions for action or requests made at the last meeting. You should be given a chance to discuss or accept these and to ask any other questions about items which appear in the minutes. Sometimes certain items will be given a separate slot for discussion later in the agenda.

Reports

LEA reports

Your LEA will send governors reports about subjects such as sex education, the curriculum or anti-racism. Sometimes these will need a decision from the governors, such as providing comments or taking action, while others are for information only.

Other reports

The governors may have asked for reports from the staff, LEA or other organisations whose work affects the school. There may be government reports or reports from governors' organisations.

Finance

All maintained schools (excluding Nursery) schools deal with most of the costs of running the school themselves. Special schools put in their schemes in April 1994. They are now funded by LMS formula but not all have control of their budget yet.

The costs will include staff, equipment, repairs, rent and rates.

The LEA must provide a report about how much money has been allocated.

If the accounting has been delegated to the headteacher, the headteacher must provide a report about how the money has been spent. (More about finance in Chapter 8.)

Headteacher's report

This is a written report from the headteacher to the governors about the school during the previous term. It should contain information about such things as:

- exam results;
- other achievements;
- staffing and staff training;
- curriculum;
- number of children in the school by age and sex;
- visits made by the staff and pupils;
- visitors to the school;
- information about health and safety in the school;
- state of the school buildings;
- use of premises by the community;
- relations with parents;
- information about any problems.

Ideally the report should be circulated to the governors before the meeting so that they can prepare questions.

Governors' reports

This agenda item provides an opportunity for governors who have visited the school to report back to their fellow governors. The report could be a spoken one, but it is better if possible to write it and hand it round at the meeting.

You can include such things as your impressions of the state of the buildings, school meals, playtime supervision, atmosphere (see also Chapter 3). Be positive first before you make any criticisms. Keep your report short and to the point.

Remember you are not expected to comment on a teacher's performance. This is the job of the LEA's school inspector or advisor. If you are concerned about standards in school you can ask for a visit from the inspector.

Other agenda items

Prizes

Not every school awards prizes but if yours does the headteacher should give details of the prizes, what they are for and what they cost, and discuss who will present them and when.

Confidential business

For any item under this heading the chairman will ask all observers to leave the room. This section is usually reserved for discussion of individuals, and items such as pupil exclusions would come under this heading.

Staff appointments

If there have been any staff changes or there are vacancies which will need to be advertised then they will be mentioned at this point.

Exclusion of pupils

The headteacher will give details of any pupils suspended or excluded and why and ask for the governors' support for his or her actions. The governors can then consider this. If a full exclusion is sought then there are official procedures to go through (see Chapter 6).

Accidents to pupils

Any accident in school must be recorded at the time on special forms and details from these must be read out to the governors for comment.

Any other business
This is on the agenda so that governors can raise any urgent items. Don't try to raise important issues which should have been put on the main agenda for full discussion. If you want to get an issue considered at length ask the clerk to put it on the agenda for the next meeting.

Special speakers
From time to time the governing body might ask people to give a talk to the meeting. These might be LEA officers or officials or individuals from outside the education authority. If they can come to the meeting it is polite for the chairman to ask the governors whether the agenda can be rearranged so that the item relevant to the speaker can be taken first. This saves the speakers, who will have made a special effort to get to the meeting, from wasting their time by sitting through business which is nothing to do with them.

READING THE REPORTS

Importance of good preparation
Delays to business at a meeting are sometimes caused by governors not doing the preparation necessary by reading the material sent to them in advance.

There is no excuse for this. Don't get into the habit yourself. It rarely takes more than a couple of hours a term to read the literature, or at least the relevant bits (how to do this is discussed later in this chapter). Try to make sure that you make this amount of time available once a term. It will be well worth it.

Delays in receiving reports
The relevant documents should reach you at least a week before the meeting. You will always be told the date of the next meeting, so if you have not received anything by a week beforehand you should contact the clerk and ask for them to be sent to you at once.

Occasionally there will be reasons why papers cannot be sent to you before the meeting and you will only receive them on the day. In this case, if time cannot be found for governors to read the document straight away, or if the document is too long, then another meeting to discuss the subject might need to be called. If no one has had time to read the paper, and it is not urgent to decide on the matter, why not suggest an extra meeting yourself?

If there are continual delays in material reaching you on time then ask the chairman of the governors to raise this with the clerk.

Minutes

Read the minutes of the last meeting carefully before your first meeting. Although you will not be able to comment on much of it yet, it will give you a good idea of the problems concerning the school and the kind of decisions the governing body makes.

At later meetings you will know whether the meeting has been recorded accurately. Make a note of anything misrepresented or missed out so that these can be corrected. Make a note in the margins of any questions you want to ask. Try not to ask questions which are answered elsewhere in the papers.

Agenda items

Check the agenda to see what items will be raised. Where reports are enclosed for such items, read them.

How to digest a report

Reports can range from a single sheet to a thick document. It is possible that the reason many governors do not read material sent to them is because they are intimidated by the size of the task and simply do not know where to start.

With a long report, it is important to be organised:

1. Read the title, contents list and headings throughout to get an idea of the subject matter.
2. Read the introduction or the first few paragraphs to get an understanding of the main theme.
3. Read the summary or the last few paragraphs to understand the report's conclusions.
4. Look at the appendices and note the summaries of their conclusions.

In long reports containing sections about different types of school you can miss out the sections which are not relevant to your school.

Very long reports should have an introduction and a summary. This is not always the case, but you will soon become an expert in finding the important conclusions.

Be selective

You can't expect to read every word of every piece of paper sent to you as a governor. It is better to have a reasonable idea of the contents of most of the papers than to spend all your time reading one report in detail and then having to say 'I don't know' at the meeting when asked about the others. If you have a special interest in one subject, then you might like to read that report in greater detail if you have time.

- Knowing what is going to be discussed at the meeting and doing careful preparation will help you to be informed and therefore confident.

CHECKLIST

1. Find out where the meetings will be held.

2. Make arrangements for child-care, if necessary.

3. Read the minutes of the previous meeting.

4. Read the agenda.

5. Read the relevant parts of any reports.

6. Make notes of any questions or comments.

5
Mastering Meetings

The new governor approaching a closed door behind which sits the governing body often experiences sheer terror. The mystical 'secret society' of governors, the clique of strangers, is unnerving.

We've all gone through it: the timid knock on the door, the nervous smile on entering, and the couple of hours of terrified silence in a meeting where everyone else seems to know what is going on and be able to speak out boldly except you.

It's not really that bad. This chapter will explain how to take part in meetings without making a fool of yourself.

FIRST MEETING AND INTRODUCTIONS

Arrive in good time for your first meeting. It can be embarrassing to walk into a meeting already in progress and find a sea of faces staring at you.

Ask the nearest person who the chairman is and **introduce yourself**. A good chairman should then introduce you to the clerk and vice-chairman or one or two other governors. If this doesn't happen, ask the chairman to do so. You will then be able to put names to a few faces when the meeting starts.

If you are a parent governor you might be nervous about meeting the school staff in a meeting as a governor rather than a parent. Don't be. As a governor you are their equal and in any case staff often are much more relaxed and approachable outside school hours.

PEOPLE PRESENT

The people at the meeting will be:

- chairman;
- vice-chairman;
- clerk to the governors;
- local authority (LEA) governors;

- teacher governors;
- headteacher (if she or he chooses to be a governor);
- parent governors;

Other people might include:

- LEA officer or official to give a report or advice;
- observers;
- deputy head;
- people especially invited by the governors or who have asked to address the governing body.

Quorum

The quorum of a meeting is the minimum number of members, in this case governors, who must be present before the meeting can officially take place and decisions can be taken. This is to stop important decisions being taken by just one or two governors who may not represent the views of the majority.

The quorum of the meeting is laid down by the LEAs individually. The quorum is usually three governors or one-third of the governing body to the nearest whole number, whichever is the larger. So a governing body with twenty members would have a quorum of seven. Individual LEAs can decide upon a larger quorum of up to two-fifths of the governing body. Three-quarters of the governors must be present to co-opt or appoint other governors.

If the number of governors present at a meeting does not meet the quorum, the chairman can decide to abandon the meeting or continue with it but make sure that everyone realises that no decisions can be taken. This could be counter-productive because at the next meeting with a quorum, governors who were not present could insist on discussing the issues again. It may, however, be the only way to discuss urgent business.

Officers

The three officers of a governing body are:

- chairman;
- vice-chairman;
- clerk to the governors.

Chairman

The chairman is the key figure in any governors meeting. The chairman is elected each year at the Annual General Meeting (AGM). It is the chairman's job to:

- introduce the items on the agenda;

- control any discussion;

- decide on points of order;

- act with the authority of the governing body outside meetings;

- act as a link between the public or LEA and the governors.

A strong chairman can make a meeting run smoothly and efficiently; a poor one will allow the meeting to ramble on and let a few people do all the talking.

The chairman should make sure that everyone is given a chance to speak and that individuals don't dominate the meeting. The chairman should draw the discussion to an end by summing up the main points and expressing the general view reached. A vote will be taken if necessary.

Although you may not wish to vote for a chairman at your first AGM because you do not know the people there, you should make a note of the kind of person who has been elected and what qualities the other governors have to offer. You might even wish to stand as chairman yourself one day—if you do, be a good one.

Vice-chairman

The vice-chairman is also elected at the AGM and deputises for the chairman when the chairman can't be present. The vice-chairman has a positive role to play at a meeting by sitting next to the chairman and offering advice or drawing the chairman's attention to governors wishing to speak.

The vice-chairman should also attend other meetings with the chairman, such as discussions with the headteacher, and contribute to any discussion or decision-making.

A good chairman will try to include the vice-chairman in these extra meetings and keep him or her up to date on what is going on. This is not only sensible so that the vice-chairman is prepared to step into the chairman's shoes at a moment's notice, but a courtesy because the vice-chairman's role is regarded as a learning role for chairman.

Clerk to the governors

The clerk usually sits on the other side of the chairman. The clerk is often an LEA officer who will be paid by the LEA. She or he will be representing the Chief Education Officer and as such will be entitled to attend all governors meetings.

However, sometimes the clerk is someone from outside the school or a teacher, parent or LEA governor. This is more common in Voluntary schools. If the clerk is also a governor, she or he is entitled to vote.

The clerk's job is to:

- take the minutes (record the notes) of any meeting;

- send out the agenda, minutes and any other relevant documents to the governors at least a week before any meeting;

- write letters on behalf of the governing body;

- provide information about current rules and regulations (an LEA clerk is in a better position to do this);

- ask for extra information needed by the governors from the relevant people;

- keep a record of all letters and documents relevant to the governing body;

- take charge of the election of the chairman;

- help governors frame resolutions (motions);

- report back to the meeting about what happened to the resolutions.

A good clerk is a boon to any meeting and a vital member of it. A poor one can slow up the business of the meeting considerably.

Observers

These are any people who wish to listen to the meeting, and they are present at the discretion of the governing body. They are not allowed to speak to the meeting without special permission from the chairman, nor to vote. If they disrupt the meeting the chairman can order them to leave.

Some of the business at a governors meeting might be confidential, for example, concerning an individual pupil. If an item on the agenda is confidential then the chairman will ask the observers to leave while that item is being discussed.

HOW MEETINGS ARE RUN

Elections

If there are any elections to take place, for example at the AGM, these will happen first. The clerk will take the nominations and record the vote for the chairman's job and then the chairman will do so for the vice-chairman.

Apologies and minutes

The chairman will welcome any new governors and then read out the names of anyone who has sent apologies for absence. The minutes of the last meeting will already have been sent to you to read. The chairman will ask if these are a correct record of the last meeting. If some people think they are not, the clerk will amend his copy of the minutes. When everyone agrees that they represent a true record of the last meeting the chairman will sign the (possibly amended) copy and give them to the clerk.

If there are any matters arising from the minutes the chairman will ask the clerk to comment on these and allow discussion.

Agenda items

After that the chairman will go through the agenda allowing time for discussion on each item and taking a vote if necessary. If no discussion is needed, then an item can be taken as 'for information only' and recorded as 'received'.

It is the chairman's job to introduce any visiting speakers, ask for questions, monitor the discussion, and thank the visitor.

If items need to be rearranged on the agenda, the chairman will do this with the permission of the governors. He or she will control any discussion and encourage everyone to speak.

Note: further reading
For a more detailed look at how meetings are run and the role of the officers, read *Citrine's ABC of Chairmanship* edited by Michael Cannell and Norman Citrine (NCLC Publishing, 1982).

TAKING PART

Speaking

In order to speak at a meeting you should catch the chairman's eye by raising your hand or pen. (Don't raise your arm right up as if you were in a classroom—even if you are!)

The Chairman should then call you to speak in turn. He or she should also stop other governors interrupting you.

Everybody gets nervous about speaking in meetings, especially for the first time. Remember the following guidelines:

- Speaking will be easier if you have made a few notes during the discussion.

- Keep your speech short and to the point.

- If you want to address someone, address the chairman: 'Chairman, I think that . . .'. It may sound odd but it is correct. The chairman represents the whole governing body which is why you address your remarks to him or her. It also helps you to address yourself to one person.

- To ask a question, proceed in the same way. Try not to ask the obvious or anything already in the papers you have been given or you will just exasperate people (see Fig. 11).

'Has the Chief Education Officer or his deputy been to see the state of these school buildings?'

'What is being done to provide the staff with anti-racist awareness training?'

'Would the head please explain the reasons for the poor exam results this year?'

'Would the teacher governor please tell us how the staff are coping with the recommendations for special educational needs within the school?'

'Is the school fully implementing the National Curriculum?'

'Why haven't the boys' toilets been repaired yet?'

'What are the staffing prospects for next term?'

'Could we reduce expenditure on computers and buy the replacement books needed after the lab fire?'

Fig. 11. Model questions.

You may not want to say anything for the first few meetings while you get your bearings. Don't be afraid to listen quietly and make notes. Sooner or later, however, you will want to speak in order to play a full part in the meeting and make sure that your point of view is heard.

Remember that although other governors may have been attending meetings for longer than you have, they do not necessarily know more than you do. In fact, if you have read your documents, paid attention on your first visit to the school and talked to the head-teacher you may well be more up to date than someone who has not done their preparation or who hasn't made a recent visit to the school.

Resolutions

Resolutions (or motions) are statements which commit the governing body to a course of action. They are 'put forward' or 'proposed'. Someone who puts forward a resolution is the **proposer**. A resolution must have at least one other person to support it. The person who supports the resolution is called the **seconder**. The clerk will make a note of the proposer's and seconder's names.

Resolutions take the form: 'I propose that . . .(the governing body takes a course of action).' (See Fig. 12.) If someone seconds the resolution it must be discussed and a vote taken. If the resolution is passed then the governing body is committed to do whatever has been proposed.

The clerk has to make an accurate record of the words of the resolution so it is a good idea to write it down first.

Voting

All governors present at a meeting are entitled to vote. If you decide that in all honesty you cannot vote a definite yes or no then you can **abstain** by not voting at all. The clerk will record abstentions as well as the for and against votes. If you wish to be on record as having voted a particular way, then you can ask the clerk to record your name by your vote.

Growing in confidence

Your first meeting is one at which you will put names to faces, get to know how the meeting is conducted and learn about what sort of business concerns the governing body. In following meetings you will become more confident about expressing your views and will begin to take a more active part in the procedure.

Declaring an interest

If you are affected by the subject under discussion—for example if you might gain financially, if you are related to a person under discussion or if you are a staff governor whose successor is under discussion—then you must 'declare your interest' in it. You must then leave the meeting until discussion of that item has finished in case you influence the discussion unfairly.

PROBLEMS

Awkward moments

There will undoubtedly be governors who try to take over the discussion, interrupt the speakers or refuse to stop talking. A strong chairman will deal with them. If someone interrupts you, do not address them directly but say to the chairman, 'Chairman, may I finish?' The chairman should then order the other person to wait their turn.

Don't be intimidated by such people. If the chairman is slow in quelling the interruption or is ineffective, address the person concerned with 'Allow me to finish please' and then continue firmly. And try to avoid interrupting other speakers yourself.

I propose that this governing body . . .

'invites the school's architect to discuss the alternatives suggested for internal structural reorganisation of the school.'

'forms a subcommittee to prepare a report on the feasibility of teaching sex education in the school.'

'sends representatives to the CEO to discuss the staffing crisis.'

'writes to Mr Brown expressing our appreciation for his sterling service as caretaker for fifteen years.'

'invites the chairman of the education committee to address the next Annual Parents Meeting.'

'ballots the parents on whether the school should become grant-maintained.'

Fig. 12. Model resolutions.

Trouble with the clerk

The clerk is vital to the governing body. Most clerks are very hard working and efficient and do an excellent job. They go to great lengths to ease the governors' work-load.

However, occasionally a governing body will get a clerk who proves unsatisfactory. If it is another governor or someone from outside, the chairman or the headteacher could have a word with them. If the clerk is an LEA officer then the chairman should voice his worries to the clerk's superior officer. The LEA is obliged to consider replacing an LEA clerk if the governors ask it to do so.

It is difficult for governors to complain about a clerk directly face to face at a meeting. Concern could be expressed in an oblique way: 'I'm concerned that we never seem to get the papers for the meetings on time' rather than 'Why don't you send our papers out on time?' This will give the clerk a chance to offer an explanation. If this is unsatisfactory the chairman can approach the clerk's superior.

Usually a quiet word from above is all that is required. If there is a genuine problem outside the clerk's control, this can be sorted out. In extreme cases the LEA clerk can be replaced. It can be tactfully suggested to non-LEA clerks that the work-load might be too much for them.

Of course, if tact doesn't work then bluntness will have to do, but in a non-aggressive manner.

Long meetings and extra meetings

Long meetings do sometimes need to take place, but it is not a good idea for them to go on for too long. Your concentration wanes and people get irritable. Decisions made under these conditions are not as carefully considered as they should be and tempers can get frayed. Meetings may end up as slanging matches or governors may decide on courses of action which they would normally have considered unwise.

If the chairman decides to end the meeting before the business is finished the governors must have another meeting to finish it. In addition, any three governors can call an extra meeting by putting their request to the chairman and the clerk. The effectiveness of such extra meetings depends on the willingness and ability of governors to turn up at them. If the minimum number of governors needed for decisions to be taken do not turn up (see **quorum**, above), then the effort has been wasted and the topics go on getting deferred.

Sometimes the subject simply gets added to the next agenda. However, this can go on for ages with the agenda getting ever longer, the time for business never being adequate to cope with the expanding list and the subject not getting discussed.

Where a deadline is indicated, an extra meeting, or an extra long meeting, to cover the subject is sometimes the only course.

- Meetings loom large in the life of a school governor. Prepare for them, participate in them, enjoy them!

CHECKLIST

1. Read and digest the papers sent to you before any meeting.

2. Get to meetings on time, particularly your first meeting.

3. Introduce yourself to the chairman at your first meeting.

4. Listen and watch until you have got the hang of how the meetings work.

5. Make notes.

6. When you want to speak catch the chairman's eye, address the chairman and speak clearly.

7. Don't be put off by pushy governors.

8. Remember that parent governors have equal rights and responsibilities to other governors.

9. Why not stand as chairman or vice-chairman—you can do it!

10. Remember—preparation, participation, enjoyment.

6
Responsibilities and Rights

Governors must do certain things and may do certain other things. These are the responsibilities and rights of the governing body and are set out in the Instrument and Articles of Government provided to every new governor.

Responsibilities—these are the things which a governing body must do and which are defined in various Education Acts.

Rights—these are the things which a governing body can do if it so decides.

RESPONSIBILITIES:

CONDUCT OF THE SCHOOL

This concerns how a County, Voluntary or maintained Special school is run. The conduct of the school is under the direction of the governing body, although the headteacher has responsibility for the day-to-day running of the school.

The headteacher or the LEA should consult the governing body before making any changes. If the chairman or vice-chairman of the governors is not available, and the matter is urgent, then the head-teacher or LEA may act without consulting the governors.

CURRICULUM

The LEA has to provide the governing body with a copy of its statement concerning the secular curriculum (that is, all subjects except religious education) in County, Voluntary and maintained Special schools.

The governing body must consider this and decide whether it agrees with it, bearing in mind the **LEA's policy** and the demands of the **National Curriculum**.

The governors must decide whether the LEA's policy should be modified for their school and must consult with the headteacher about it. They must also take into account the views of people from the local community and the chief of police in the area. (See Chapter 9 for more information about the curriculum.)

When they have reviewed the policy, the governors must write their own statement and give a copy to the LEA and the head-teacher. The headteacher must show it to anyone with a reasonable wish to see it.

The governors must inform the parents about any syllabuses to be followed by the pupils in the school.

Sex education

Sex education is part of the secular curriculum and must be con-sidered separately. The governors must decide whether sex educa-tion should be taught in their school and write a statement giving their reasons for or against it. This statement must also be given to the LEA and headteacher.

When sex education is to be taught the governors must ensure, as far as possible, that it is done to encourage pupils 'to have due regard to moral considerations and the value of family life' (EA 86).

Political indoctrination

The governors, headteacher and LEA must not allow teachers to teach in a way which gives children politically biased views. Junior school children are not allowed to take part in politically biased activities in school, or out of school if these are arranged by a staff member.

Where political issues are put forward at school or during a school's official extra-curricular activities, these must be presented in a balanced way.

DISCIPLINE

The governing body must provide a written statement of general principles regarding discipline in the school and offer guidance in relation to particular matters.

It is the job of the headteacher, however, to decide how the discipline of the pupils in the school is to be achieved, and this can include the making and enforcing of rules. The headteacher must make it clear throughout the school how discipline is to be obtained and set the standard of behaviour. The headteacher may also exclude pupils. Corporal punishment is against the law in maintained schools.

When organising disciplinary measures the headteacher must be guided by the written statement from the governors and take note of any advice they may give on particular issues.

Governors and headteachers will need to take into account government advice issued in January 1994. This recommends punishment by detentions, barring from sports events or school trips, public or private rebukes and letters to parents. It suggests praise by merit marks, public commendation in assembly and displays of good work. Most schools will already operate similar systems. If any means of discipline will cost the LEA money or affect its position as an employer, then the governors and the headteacher must consult the LEA before introducing such measures.

Exclusion of pupils

In County, Voluntary and maintained Special schools, only the headteacher has the right to exclude (suspend) pupils from school, that is, to forbid the pupil to come to school either for a short or indefinite period or permanently. In the advice issued by the government in January 1994 exclusions are frowned upon except as a last resort for persistent troublemakers. It recommends that pupils should *not* be excluded for occasional swearing, not doing homework, not bringing dinner money, being pregnant or failing to comply with uniform regulations for cultural, religious or financial reasons. Pupils *may* be excluded for repeated smoking, drinking on premises, drug taking or trafficking, bullying, assault causing injury, use of weapons, sexual assault and arson. The headteacher must tell the pupil's parents about an exclusion as soon as possible so that they can if they wish appeal to the governing body and LEA. (If the pupil is over eighteen then it is the pupil who must be told.)

The governors and the LEA must be told about any exclusion which would mean a pupil being absent from school for five or more days in a term or missing a public exam, or if a temporary exclusion is made permanent. The headteacher must give reasons for the exclusion.

When a child has been permanently excluded then the LEA must consult the governors about it before deciding whether to reinstate the pupil or not.

When a pupil has been excluded for five or more days or may miss an exam then the headteacher must abide by the LEA's ruling when the period of exclusion is fixed, and otherwise by the ruling of the governing body.

The LEA can overrule the governors when a pupil has been excluded indefinitely unless the headteacher decides otherwise.

When the LEA and governors give different orders about a pupil's exclusion, then the headteacher must obey whoever has decided on the earlier reinstatement of the pupil.

In Aided and Special Agreement schools it is the responsibility of the governing body to decide whether an exclusion continues and, when they decide it should be permanent, to inform the LEA.

Appeals

Every LEA must have arrangements so that parents of pupils who have been permanently excluded (or the pupils themselves if over eighteen) can appeal against the exclusion. They must also let governing bodies appeal against reinstatements when the headteacher of their school has been directed to reinstate a pupil by the LEA.

Any decision by an appeals committee is binding.

FINANCE

All schools now have schemes for **Local Management of Schools** (LMS). (Nursery schools are not included). Schools are now responsible for managing their own budgets.

Special schools were included in the schemes from April 1994.

LMS means that the school is allocated a lump sum with which to pay for all resources, staff, equipment, buildings, and so on. The governors have the final responsibility for managing the budget, even though they may delegate it to the headteacher.

The LEA allocates the budget to the school, but it is up to the governors how it is spent. Grant-maintained schools and CTCs receive their money from the government (through the Funding Agency for Schools (FAS)). The governors are accountable for how the money is spent and must report on this to parents in their Annual Report.

More information about how to cope with a budget is found in Chapter 8.

ANNUAL REPORT TO PARENTS

Each year the governors must provide a brief written report to all parents explaining how they have carried out their duties during the past year. They must then hold a meeting for all parents in order to discuss the report.

The report must contain:

• details of the time, place and agenda of the meeting.

• an explanation of the purpose of the meeting—that is, to discuss the governors' report.

- the name of each governor and what kind of governor they are; for example, Foundation, Parent.

- details of who appointed each governor; for example, LEA.

- name and address of the chairman of the governors and the clerk to the governors.

- information about the next election of parent governors.

- a summary of the latest financial statement given to the governors by the LEA, explaining generally how any money available to the governing body from the LEA has been spent. Any gifts to the school should be mentioned too.

- for Secondary Schools—details of public examinations taken by pupils of the school.

- the steps taken to improve the school's links with the local community and the police.

- a statement about any decision to ballot or not on grant-maintained status.

The report can be produced in any languages which the governors consider sensible. It must be produced in a language other than English if the LEA says so.

All parents of pupils registered at the school must receive a copy of the report at least two weeks before the Annual Parents Meeting.

Annual Parents Meeting

The governors must hold a meeting once a year for all parents of children registered at the school, the headteacher and anyone else invited by the governing body. The purpose of the meeting is to discuss the governors' report and how the governors, headteacher and LEA have carried out their duties to the school.

The governing body will be in charge of the running of the meeting. When the number of parents present at the meeting is equal to 20 per cent of the pupils registered at the school, the meeting can pass resolutions by a simple majority about anything which can be properly discussed at the meeting. The governing body must consider any such resolution and give the headteacher and LEA copies of resolutions which concern them. The headteacher and LEA must consider any such resolutions and give the governors a brief written comment on it to include in the next governors' report.

When the governors of a Special school in a hospital decide it is not sensible to hold an Annual Parents Meeting in a particular year they do not need to do so.

The Annual Parents Meeting is a very important event for governors because it is a chance for parents and governors to talk about the concerns of the school. Try to get to it.

ADMISSIONS

Every year the LEA must publish details of its admissions policy. Where the LEA is responsible for deciding the admissions policy in a County or Voluntary school, it must consult the governors every year as to whether it is satisfactory. The LEA must also consult the governors if they wish to alter the admissions policy. The governors must consult the LEA for the same reasons where the governing body decides the admissions arrangements.

Schools now have to admit pupils up to a **standard number** decided by the Secretary of State. If a school wants to change its standard number it must apply to the Secretary of State. The standard number is related to the number of pupils a school can hold.

Parents can choose which school to send their child to and can appeal to the LEA if their child is not given a place. The LEA's admissions policy must explain which children get priority if the school does not have enough places for all who apply.

An important job for the governors is to make sure that the school has an up-to-date record of the number of pupils at the school.

STAFF APPOINTMENTS AND DISMISSALS

Now that most schools have to manage their own budgets, the governing body is responsible for the hiring and firing and disciplining of all staff—teaching and non-teaching.

The governors can decide:

• how many staff to appoint (within their budget);

• what grades the staff will be (within their budget);

• what the disciplinary procedures will be;

• what the grievance procedures will be;

- suspensions;

- dismissals.

The Chief Education Officer (CEO) of the LEA has the right to attend governors meetings and give advice about appointment and dismissal of teachers—either for all teachers or just headteachers and deputy headteachers. This will depend on what agreement the governors have made with the LEA or what the Secretary of State has decided for that school.

The LEA will advise the governors about dismissal procedures. If the governors dismiss any staff they must inform the LEA and give reasons for dismissal. If the governors follow the dismissal procedures given by the LEA then they will not have to pay any costs relating to the dismissal, such as redundancy pay. These will be paid by the LEA.

Governors are responsible for interviewing all staff for appointments. Information about interviewing staff is given in Chapter 7.

SCHOOL PREMISES

The governors have the power to decide how the school premises shall be used when the school is not in session. They must bear in mind that it is a good thing for the local community to use the school premises when the school does not need them.

The governors can decide who will use the premises, and fix times and fees.

DISCRIMINATION AND EQUAL OPPORTUNITIES

Sex discrimination

By law boys and girls must not be treated differently because of their sex. There must be no sex discrimination in admission to schools and boys and girls must be given equal access to courses and facilities (Sex Discrimination Act 1975).

Governors must ensure that the school does not operate any practices which discriminate between the sexes. It should be clear that although most people think of sexism in terms of male discrimination against females, the opposite is just as true and equally illegal.

Sexism can be obvious, such as only letting boys use the computers or making girls clear up the classroom. It can also be hidden and only be evident in people's attitudes; for example, a teacher may always ask the boys questions or the school may provide facilities which are supposed to be open to all pupils but make it difficult for one sex to use them.

Sexism may also be evident in the role models provided by the school itself. For example, do only the male teachers take outdoor sports lessons? Are the books the children use showing outdated stereotypes such as the boys always being the gang leaders and the girls playing with dolls? Shouldn't girls play football and boys hockey? Why shouldn't girls wear trousers?

Where subject choices have to be made, girls and boys should be allowed equal access to the subjects available and be given the same quality of careers guidance.

Governors should have a clear policy on sexism and make sure that the staff and parents are aware of it.

Race discrimination

Much of what has been said about sex discrimination can be said about race discrimination. Discrimination on the grounds of race is illegal (Race Relations Act 1976). Although people think that black children are most likely to be the butt of race discrimination, other children can and do suffer discrimination on the grounds of race. The law applies equally to them.

Teachers and governors must ensure that attitudes and practices in the school give no grounds for a charge of racism. Particular events such as bullying must be dealt with promptly and fairly. Remember, too, that some children suffer both sex and race discrimination and incidents involving such children must be handled sensitively.

Governors must have a policy on racism and make it available to all staff and parents (see Fig. 13). Many schools have arranged for staff to take part in sexism and racism awareness courses. This should be something for your school to consider doing.

It is important with both racism and sexism to be aware that the attitudes and practices of non-teaching staff are just as important in determining how the children are treated and perceived by others and so they should be included in any relevant training programme.

Equal opportunities

While children should not be treated any differently because of race or sex, they should also be given the same educational opportunities. This means, for example, that girls should be given access to metal workshops and computers and boys to cookery and needlework. Sports should be made equally available too.

Equal opportunities and anti-discrimination statement

This school believes in the right of every individual to be treated with respect and to enjoy freedom of expression and equal opportunities.

This school will not tolerate discrimination against any individual on the grounds of race or ethnic origin, gender, class, age, ability, language, sexual orientation, physical disability, physical appearance or status.

We recognise that prejudice exists in our society and will demonstrate that we will not tolerate this by treating seriously and acting promptly against any form of discriminatory behaviour.

This school is fully committed to nurturing a climate of mutual respect within the school and to ensuring that all pupils are given equal help and encouragement and access to the opportunities available.

Fig. 13. Model equal opportunities and anti-discrimination statement.

Apart from breaking down traditional assumptions about abilities and interests, all children must be given the same opportunities. This means that no one must be excluded from advice—it should no longer be the case that girls are only advised to go into nursing, teaching or the civil service and boys are told to be lawyers or engineers.

Governors should ensure that they have a policy on equal opportunities and that they ensure that all the children in the school are given access to all the educational advantages available, without prejudice.

RIGHTS

Becoming Grant-Maintained

Any County or Voluntary school, unless discontinued, can now decide whether to apply to the Secretary of State to '**opt out**' of the state system and become a grant-maintained school. If the Secretary of State gives the school permission to become grant-maintained, then the school will receive money directly from the government through the Funding Agency for Schools. The sum it gets will be equivalent to the sum received by the LEA for a similar state-maintained school. It will be based on a per capita allowance, that is, a sum of money for each pupil in the school. Therefore the more pupils such a school has, the more money it will receive.

Now the Funding Agency functions LEAs cannot establish grant-maintained schools and this is the job of the Funding Agency and promotors. A grant-maintained school is independent of the LEA.

Consultation on 'opting-out' is very important. Governors and parents can be in conflict over this issue. Each year Governors must consider holding a ballot on grant-maintained status, unless a ballot was held the previous year. The Annual Report to parents must include a statement about whether balloting has been considered and record any decisions and reasons for or against holding such a ballot.

There are certain **stages** which must be gone through before a school can obtain grant-maintained status:

1. The governors decide to ballot all parents about opting out. This can be done if the governors pass a resolution to do so. They must hold a ballot if they receive a written request to do so from parents equal in number to at least 20 per cent of the pupils registered at the school.
2. The governing body consults the LEA if it is a maintained school, or the Trustees if it is a Voluntary school.
3. The governors confirm the decision to ballot the parents in a resolution passed between twenty-eight and forty-two days of the first resolution.
4. A secret ballot is held of all parents with pupils registered at the school. Parents can ask to have a school list of all registered parents except those who have asked for their names and address to be kept secret. The governors can charge the parents for this list. The governing body can promote the case for grant-maintained status. But the ballot may declared invalid if voters are given false or misleading information. The information given to each parent must be enough for him or her to make a reasoned judgement about whether it is a good idea to opt out. The information must include, for example, how the school would become grant-maintained, the consequences, who the new governors would be (see Fig. 14) and on what date the new system would be expected to start.

    If less than 50 per cent of the people eligible to vote do so then another ballot must be held within fourteen days. The Secretary of State for Education can declare a ballot void and order a reballot if he considers it has not been conducted fairly.

5. If a simple majority in the ballot is in favour of opting out, the governors must publish proposals for opting out and submit a copy to the Secretary of State within four months of the ballot result becoming known.
6. There is a chance to raise objections within two months of the publication of the proposals. These can come from:

- at least ten local authority voters;
- the Trustees of the school (if any);
- the governing body of any schools affected by the proposal;
- the LEA.

7. The Secretary of State will either reject the proposals, ask for modifications, or accept them.
8. If accepted, the proposals come into effect on the date specified.

KEEPING PARENTS INFORMED

The governing body is required to provide parents with certain information as set down in the Instrument and Articles of Government, in particular, the information to be given in the school prospectus, Annual Report to parents and the Annual Parents Meeting.

53–(4) The instrument of government for a grant-maintained school shall provide for the governing body to include-

(a) five parent governors;
(b) at least one but not more than two teacher governors;
(c) the person who is for the time being the head teacher (as a governor ex officio); and
(d) either-
(i) in the case of a school which was a county school immediately before it became a grant-maintained school, first governors; or
(ii) in the case of a school which was a voluntary school immediately before it became a grant-maintained school, foundation governors.

Fig. 14. Governors for a grant-maintained school—Education Reform Act 1988. (With acknowledgement to the Controller of Her Majesty's Stationery Office.)

It is, however, in the interests of the school that governors keep parents as fully informed as possible about what they are doing for the school and what decisions they have taken about it.

A lot of trouble and uncertainty can be caused from parents getting their information by way of rumour or misreporting of a situation. The best way to counter disturbance and dismay is to give the parents frequent, full and up-to-date information.

Obviously this will require more work from the governors and the headteacher in providing regular reports and letters home, but the gain in terms of trust, support and co-operation from the parents is invaluable.

Information can be given in:

- regular newssheets;
- letters home;
- parent/staff meetings;
- talks to parents by governors and/or staff;
- talks by LEA officers/councillors/education experts;
- school open days.

As a governor it is sensible to keep parents informed. Is your governing body doing as much as it could?

CHECKLIST

1. Make sure you are clear about the governors' duties concerning the conduct of the school.

2. Do you know what the LEA and governing body's policy about the curriculum is?

3. Make sure your governing body has produced a policy statement about sexism, racism, equal opportunities, sex education and discipline.

4. Do you understand the LEA's appeal procedure? Find out what it is.

5. Try to find a training course about school finance.

6. Make sure that the Annual Report to Parents contains all the information necessary. Why not volunteer to help draft it?

7. Attend the Annual Parents Meeting.

8. Can the governors involve the community by letting them use the school premises?

9. Take part in staff appointments and dismissals when given the opportunity.

10. Has your governing body discussed becoming grant-maintained and come to a decision about it?

11. Keep parents informed—the more they know, the more supportive they are likely to be.

'I don't think he's a very good role model for the teachers, dear'

7
Appointing Staff

However fine the school buildings are, however keen the children are, no school will function well without the right staff. The staff, teaching as well as non-teaching, must be qualified for the job, have the right attributes for it and, perhaps most important of all, want to work in your school.

Choosing staff is one of the governors' most important jobs. The type of staff employed decides the standard of education and ethos within the school.

WHAT PART DO GOVERNORS PLAY?

Governors play an important part in choosing staff.

Local Management of Schools

Schools now operate Local Management of Schools (**LMS**) schemes. This means that each governing body is allocated a lump sum from which they have to pay for teaching and non-teaching staff, building repairs, equipment and anything else the school needs.

So a school which used to employ several teachers with incentive allowances as well as main grade teachers may find that it can only afford probationers and a few main grade staff or has to reduce staff numbers in order to pay for other things.

Schools must also interview and appoint their own non-teaching staff.

Stages in the selection process

The governors will be involved with staff appointments. These must be handled in an efficient and fair way. The stages are as follows:

1. Draw up selection panel from among the governors.
2. Draw up job specification.
3. Advertise the post and send out application forms.

4. Take up and receive references.
5. Short list candidates.
6. Interview short-listed candidates.
7. Either make a choice or readvertise the post.

SELECTION PANEL AND ADVERTISEMENT

Selection panel

A selection panel should be chosen from among the governors, perhaps on a rota basis, to interview candidates.

When choosing a panel try to ensure that the governors are balanced in terms of sex and ethnic origin. The chairman, vice-chairman and headteacher will normally be part of this panel.

Although it is possible to delegate selection to the headteacher it is better for the governors to take a full part in the proceedings. Choosing staff is so important that governors ought to be involved as much as possible.

Job specification

It is difficult to know how to advertise the post or interview a candidate effectively unless you understand exactly what the job you are advertising entails.

A job specification gives the governors who are inspecting applications and interviewing candidates an objective guideline against which to judge how suitable a candidate is. It also gives any candidate a clear idea of what the job entails, whether they would be suitable and whether they would like the school.

The job specification should have three parts:

1. Job description.
2. Description of person needed for the job (person specification).
3. School description.

1. Job description

This should describe the duties and responsibilities of the post. It is usually drawn up by the headteacher and the school inspector or advisor and should be discussed with the governors.

The job description could include many of the following:

- title of job and what it consists of;

- any extra allowances which will be paid;

- terms and conditions of job;

- where the job will be located;

- who the post holder will be responsible to and who he or she will be working with;

- how much work the post holder will be expected to do;

- other responsibilities—for other people, finances, equipment, and so on;

- career and training prospects.

2. Description of person needed
This should include details of the skills, qualities and type of experience needed for the job. These should be relevant to the job, legal and realistic. They should not be qualities which all staff are expected to have. It may include, for example:

- education needed;

- skills needed;

- job-related training;

- relevant experience (which might have been achieved in a different sphere);

- knowledge needed;

- attitudes desirable.

It is usual for the headteacher to write the job description but the governors must see and approve it and the governors who are interviewing candidates must have a copy to hand.

3. School description
This should describe the school in realistic but positive terms. It is important that potential candidates know what sort of school they are applying to. You want to attract candidates who actually want to work in your kind of school. It is no good glossing over faults; otherwise you are wasting everybody's time. Items may include:

- description of school buildings;

- staff structure of the school;

- details of pupil intake, ages, absenteeism, and number receiving free meals;

- details of governing body;

- parent and community links;

- successes achieved by school.

Advertising the post

Governors decide whether a post should be filled. The LEA cannot insist on redeploying staff but can nominate candidates to be considered with other applicants.

The governors can decide to accept an LEA nomination, or appoint someone already working in the school. If they don't then they must advertise the post.

Individual LEAs will have their own guidelines about advertising. Governors should try to make sure that the wording is appropriate and placed to attract the best candidates (see Fig. 15). It must not be worded in a way which could be considered sexist or racist.

Applications

Any candidate for a job will be sent an application form which will ask for the candidate's name, address, work history, qualifications and experience and a statement of why they consider themselves suitable for the job. It is from these applications that a short list can be drawn up for interview.

Obviously when looking at the applications the panel must see which candidates most fit the job specification.

Short list

How many candidates are short listed depends both on LEA guidelines and on how many applicants there are. Governors may have to decide whether to interview the only candidate available or to readvertise in order to have a better selection to choose from. Some schools in less popular areas have been known to readvertise for years, even for a job such as headteacher, without attracting suitable candidates.

Ideally the minimum for a short list should be five or six, but it will be up to the governors to decide on a number. The guidelines for selecting headteachers and deputy headteachers are somewhat different and are dealt with later in the chapter.

References

These contain information about candidates from their present or most recent employer and should be obtained for all short-listed candidates.

Some references will be in the form of an open report which the candidate will have seen, others will be confidential. Governors may also receive additional testimonials or reports, open or otherwise.

References may be circulated to governors before candidates are interviewed, after each interview, or at the end when the final decisions are made.

Confidential references and reports must be treated as such. Even open reports are privileged information and should not be divulged elsewhere.

INTERVIEWS

All short-listed candidates will be invited to attend an interview at a particular time and place, usually at the school. They will be met and settled into a room near the interview room, but out of earshot of other people's interviews.

In the case of selecting a deputy headteacher or headteacher a representative of the CEO (Chief Education Officer), usually the school inspector, is entitled to attend the meeting and to offer advice.

The chairman will make sure before the interviews start that everyone present understands the procedure, any time limits set and what sort of questions may or may not be asked. Discussion of the job specification and what the governors are looking for in a candidate should have taken place at a previous meeting.

Each candidate is brought in separately. The chairman will welcome them, ask a straightforward question or two to put them at their ease and then ask for questions from the panel. The governors will ask their questions (see below). The inspector or headteacher may ask some final questions. The chairman should finally ask the candidate whether he or she would accept the post if it was offered to them. This is not as silly as it sounds. It has been known for candidates to change their minds during the interview! The chairman will thank the candidate who will then leave and make way for the next person.

It is helpful to make notes about candidates during the interview to remind you about their answers.

After all the candidates have been interviewed the headteacher and/or the inspector may wish to make a brief summing up of

Main Scale

BARKING & DAGENHAM

LONDON BOROUGH OF BARKING AND DAGENHAM
WARREN COMPREHENSIVE SCHOOL
Whalebone Lane North
Chadwell Heath, Romford
Essex
(Roll 700)
Required for September 1990.

An experienced teacher of English or a new entrant to the profession is required to join our enthusiastic and committed staff within this 11–18 years mixed comprehensive school situated on the edge of the Essex countryside and yet within easy reach of Central London. The school is easily accessible from the M11, M25, A12 and by rail.

Main Scale plus £1,500 per annum Inner London Allowance, plus an additional increment for newly appointed teachers. Probationary teacher may be appointed from 1st July 1990.

Reimbursement of removal expenses in approved cases.

Following a £3 million rebuilding programme the school is very well resourced and all teaching takes place in modern specialist rooms.

An extensive computer network provides I.T. facilities in all classrooms.

Interested applicants are welcome to visit the school. (Tel: 081–590 0435).

Applications to the school by letter with C.V. and the names and addresses of two professional referees as soon as possible.

An equal opportunity employer.

Fig. 15. Advertisement for a teacher.
(From *The Times Educational Supplement*, 4 May 1990.
Reproduced with permission of Warren Comprehensive School.)

candidates and also comment on their **references**. The LEA (or governors in schools with delegated budgets) should take up references on all short-listed candidates. Treat these with caution as not all references are open or written with adequate understanding of the candidate.

Although the governors should listen to the advice of the inspector and headteacher, in the end it is up to the governors whom they decide to appoint.

The governors will be asked for their views on the suitability of the candidates and then an agreement will be arrived at. There may well be a vote.

If a candidate has·been selected, that person will be called in and offered the post.

Questions

New governors on a selection panel often have difficulty in deciding on suitable questions to ask. Sometimes they are so nervous about asking the wrong thing that they don't ask anything at all!

It is important to remember three things:

- the questions must not be racist, sexist or in any other way discriminatory;

- questions should not invite simply a 'yes' or 'no' answer;

- each candidate should be asked broadly similar questions.

Discrimination

Even today racist or sexist questions get asked at interviews. There is no excuse for it. People who ask such questions sometimes claim to have forgotten that they are not allowed to and will normally get shouted down by the other governors. However, this is not acceptable behaviour. The chairman must rule any such questions out of order, ask for an apology and remind other governors to ignore the question.

You must not ask questions about:

- marital status
- family responsibilities
- race
- sexual orientation
- disability
- membership of organisations
- politics

'How do you approach the task of encouraging anti-racist attitudes in the classroom?'

'What skills do you have which are particularly suitable for this job?'

'Would you tell us something about how you reorganised language resources in your last school?'

'What changes would you make if you were offered the post?'

'How do you encourage parents to become involved in their child's education?'

'How would you deal with a conflict of approach between yourself and the headteacher?'

'Can you tell us something about your achievements over the past year?'

'What special qualities can you bring to this job?'

'What contribution can you bring to the school's active community involvement?'

Fig. 16. Typical questions for use when interviewing candidates for teaching posts.

You must assume that any candidate who has applied and has the necessary qualifications is able to arrange their life to get to work and is physically capable of doing the job. You must certainly not ask women questions about child-care or marital status.

Nor should these considerations arise when discussing the candidate afterwards. Comments such as 'How is he going to manage with a leg like that?' or 'Didn't she look dowdy?' (yes—it has been said) have no place in the discussion.

Open-ended questions
Questions should also be open ended. It is far more useful to ask 'Would you tell us something about how you organise your classroom for a mixed ability class?' than 'Do you find teaching a mixed

ability class difficult?' The first question gives the candidate the chance to explain about class organisation; the second simply invites the answer 'yes' or 'no'.

Similar questions for all candidates
Some schools insist that all candidates are asked exactly the same questions. This can be limiting and not necessarily fair because it might not give candidates a chance to talk about their strengths. It is perhaps better that the chairman, with the governors, should define broad topics about which the governors can ask questions to all candidates.

Encouraging good replies
Remember to keep the questions to the point and to encourage the candidate to speak. Long rambling questions from you may tell governors a lot about your opinions and prejudices but will confuse the candidate and discourage his or her reply.

The more a candidate can be encouraged to speak, the more able the governors will be to judge the candidate's suitability for the job.

This applies just as much to non-teaching staff. It is sometimes forgotten how much non-teaching staff contribute to the attitudes and practical life of the school.

Impartiality

This can be very difficult. You may well know a candidate because he or she is your child's class teacher, for example. How do you remain impartial when looking at application forms or interviewing a candidate?

This is where the job specification comes in. You must judge any candidate, whether you know them or not, by their suitability for the job. This will become more obvious as you read the applications and listen to what the candidates say in the interviews. Remember, you are not choosing someone for your own satisfaction but for the good of the school.

If, however, you feel that you cannot make a fair judgement of someone, then the only honourable course is to resign from the selection panel and let another governor take your place. You can then take a turn on a panel on another occasion.

There are, of course, occasions when you must withdraw from the panel:

- if you are or could be a candidate;

- if your relative is or could be a candidate;

- if you are a headteacher or deputy headteacher and your successor is being chosen;

- if you have a financial interest.

HEADTEACHERS AND DEPUTY HEADTEACHERS

Under LMS the governors appoint the headteacher and deputy. The governing body will set up a selection panel. The post must be advertised throughout England and Wales and anywhere where appropriate candidates may be found. The Chief Education Officer or his representative has a right to attend all meetings of the panel and governors must listen to his or her advice, but only governors can vote. Deputy headteachers can be selected by the same procedure as headteachers and the headteacher can attend all meetings when a deputy headteacher is to be appointed. The LEA must appoint the person recommended by the governors unless he or she is not legally qualified for the job or is physically or educationally unfit for the job.

NON-TEACHING STAFF

The governors interview and choose non-teaching staff. The LEA must appoint whoever is chosen by the governors, unless they do not meet the legal requirements of the job. If the job involves more than sixteen hours work, the governors must consult the headteacher and the CEO before recommending someone.

CLERK TO THE GOVERNORS

The governing body can choose a clerk if the position is vacant. The governors should consult the CEO who can offer advice. The LEA must appoint the clerk chosen by the governors.

ROLE OF CHAIRMAN AND INSPECTOR

Chairman's role
The chairman of the governors has to oversee the choosing of the selection panel and the running of the interview meeting. It is the chairman's job to make sure that the selection panel is representative of the governors and that any governor who wishes to take part in a selection procedure gets a chance to do so at some point.

The chairman must ensure the smooth running of the interviews by making sure that governors understand the procedure and have questions prepared. He or she must ensure that all candidates are welcomed, given the same amount of time for their interview and are asked broadly similar questions.

At the end of the interviews the chairman will thank the candidate. He or she will also oversee the discussion by the governors afterwards and make sure that it is kept relevant and fair and reaches a conclusion.

When the chosen candidate is called in (if there is one) the chairman will offer him or her the post and, assuming it is accepted, the congratulations of the governors.

The inspector's role

The school inspector or advisor attends selection meetings as the representative of the CEO. He or she can offer advice to the governors and may wish to sum up and comment on candidates after interviews. It is up to the governors to decide whether to accept this advice although they must take it into consideration.

The inspector or the headteacher should talk to rejected candidates immediately after the interviews so that they do not leave without seeing anyone.

CONDITIONS OF EMPLOYMENT AND DISMISSAL PROCEDURES

Pay and conditions

Teachers have their pay and conditions set by law. Existing staff (teaching and non-teaching) have contracts with extra provisions which have been agreed locally and nationally.

Schools are now responsible for deciding whether to pay staff extra money as 'incentive allowances' for extra duties or good quality teaching. The governors must draw up a list of reasons for giving an allowance so that it is seen to be done fairly.

When non-teaching staff are newly appointed the governors in these schools can decide what grade to appoint at.

Staff dismissal

Under LMS it is the governors who dismiss the staff employed solely at the school. The LEA must issue a notice of dismissal within fourteen days of being notified.

The person being dismissed must have the right to make representations to the governors before a decision is taken. He or she must have the right to appeal before the decision is sent to the LEA.

The CEO has the right to be present or represented at dismissal proceedings. If the person being dismissed appeals to the Industrial Tribunal the governing body must appear to defend its decision.

Disciplinary and grievance procedures

The governing body must set out rules for disciplinary action against staff and procedures for staff to follow if they have a grievance about their job. All the staff must be told about these rules and procedures.

Suspensions

The governing body and the headteacher can suspend a member of staff on full pay and must tell each other and the LEA.

Only the governing body can end the suspension.

- Try to take part in choosing staff. It is the staff who will make or break the school and it is your duty to make sure that the children in the school are taught and looked after by the best people possible.

CHECKLIST

1. Consult your Articles of Government to see who should be on a staff selection committee.

2. Agree on a job specification.

3. Approve the advertisement for the job.

4. Study the references of short-listed candidates when you receive them.

5. Short list candidates according to the job specification.

6. Interview short-listed candidates.

7. Consider the advice of the inspector and headteacher.

8. Choose someone for the job or decide to readvertise the post.

8
How To Manage the Money

Nothing brings a blank look on to governors' faces quicker than the finance item on the agenda. It is a relief to many governing bodies to delegate the responsibility for the school's finances to the head-teacher, to nod wisely when he or she produces the budget for the next year and to agree the LEA report on the school's allocation of money as 'received' without understanding it. But they could not be making a bigger mistake.

Even if the headteacher has done all the work, it is the governors who are responsible for the money. You don't want to be accused of agreeing to some unsuitable use of the money because you haven't bothered to understand it.

However nervous you are about the thought of budgets and finance in general, you have a responsibility to understand and comment on the financial situation for your school. Governors have to report to the parents on the way the school has been spending the money. They must show this in the Annual Report to Parents and be able to answer questions about it at the Annual Parents Meeting.

Don't despair. You won't have to sign the cheques, nor will you necessarily have to draw up a budget. You will have to understand enough to be able to decide whether you agree with the way the money is being spent.

Understanding a budget is not difficult. If you can manage the housekeeping or understand your bank statement then you can understand the school budget. The sums may be different but the principle is the same.

What is a budget?
A budget is a statement of how you are going to spend what money you have. When your school is allocated money by the LEA, the governing body must decide how the money will be spent and write it down—a budget statement.

Once the budget has been agreed, it will be the document against which the school's expenditure during the year will be assessed. It is the way to check whether the school is over- or under-spending or spending on things that were not agreed.

SOURCES AND AMOUNTS

Where does the money come from?

The money for your school to spend will come from your LEA. Your LEA, as part of the Local Authority, gets most of its money from the council tax, rates on businesses, central government grants, as well as other fees and charges. The LEA then allocates money to each school. Schools which have 'opted out' to become grant-maintained schools (see Chapter 6) will receive similar amounts but directly from the Government through the FAS.

Individual schools can raise extra money, the 'school fund', from, for example, donations, sales and letting school premises.

All maintained schools (except Nursery Schools) have the power to deal with virtually all the money needed to run their schools. This is called Local Management of Schools (LMS—see below).

How can you be effective as a governor if you have no idea how the school's money is being spent and whether it is wisely spent?

When will your school get the money?

Most LEAs will plan for money to be allocated and spent during a financial year, that is from April to March. This means that the governors have to plan for the school year from September to August but start the spending in April. Obviously careful planning must go into every budget to make sure that the money is spent sensibly across the year.

How much will your school get?

Your governing body has full financial control of your school. This means that you will have a **delegated budget**.

Each LEA has to work out an easy to understand formula to decide how much money a school needs to run effectively. Eighty per cent of this sum is an amount based on the number of pupils for each age group in the school and includes extra allowances for pupils with Special Educational Needs and for small schools.

Having a delegated budget means that your governing body will be responsible for such areas as:

• teaching staff;

• non-teaching staff;

- rent and rates

- building—internal maintenance;

- equipment—including furniture and fittings as well as educational equipment;

- fuel and light;

- books, stationery;

- office needs—such as postage, telephone and printing;

- school visits and staff travel;

- exam fees;

- cleaning materials and equipment.

The LEA still keeps control of grants from central government as well as a certain part of the money which is needed for central services, such as advisory services, and major building items. Your LEA may decide to keep control of other areas such as the school meal service but it can only hold back a limited amount of the money it must delegate for schools to spend. (For a guide to the LMS system read *Local Management of Schools* by Brent Davies & Chris Braund, Northcote House, 1989).

With a delegated budget you have a great responsibility. You will have to decide how the money for everything in the school is to be spent. It is possible to delegate this to the headteacher and many schools will no doubt do so, but the governors have the final responsibility for how the money for their school is spent.

Role of headteacher
You may think that it is a good idea to leave managing the money to the headteacher. He or she will certainly have a good idea about what the money could or should be spent on. However, don't let the headteacher get away with spending money in a way which you disagree with. If you feel strongly about how the money is to be spent then you must speak up about it. It is part of a governor's job to express an opinion on any school budget.

Role of LEA
If the LEA decides that a governing body is not dealing with a delegated budget in a responsible manner it can suspend its right to

manage the budget by giving the governing body one month's notice.

In fact one school turned this rule on its head and simply refused to take on the responsibility of a delegated budget, much to the LEA's consternation.

Your LEA will, of course, give help and guidance to your governing body about money management, staffing needs, and so on.

UNDERSTANDING A BUDGET

Whatever amount of money the governing body is in control of, it will be necessary to understand a budget.

Schools have to draw up a budget statement showing how they will spend the money. This will include major items such as staff and internal maintenance of school buildings.

Income and expenditure

First of all you have to know your income. Your LEA will tell the governing body exactly how much is in the school's budget. Then you must decide what to spend on which items.

When you are looking at a budget statement the expenditure should be the same or less than the income. When a school writes its own budget statement, income and expenses should be separately and clearly set out.

Let us take a simple example. Suppose the governors of a small school allocate £3,000 of their overall budget for equipment. The headteacher may suggest spending £1,000 on a new computer and software, £1,000 on books, and £1,000 on stationery and printing.

Income		Expenditure	
	£3000	Computer	£1000
		Books	£1000
		Stationery	£1000
	£3000		£3000

As you can see this adds up to the £3,000 allocated. Like any good housekeeper you cannot spend more than you have. You, as governors, cannot spend more than the budget for your school.

However, even a simple budget statement must be looked at closely. Suppose your school already has several computers that are not fully used. Should you then spend the money allocated for computers on more books? You, the governor, must have an opinion on this.

Role of governors

The governing body can delegate responsibility for their budget to the headteacher, but many more will want to take part in the process by allocating one or more governors to draw up the budget in consultation with the headteacher. In any case, any budget must be approved by the whole governing body.

The LEA will tell you how much money you can spend, for example, £1,963,000. The sums of money are very large but the principle is clear. You cannot spend more than you have.

Of course, this need to keep within the allowed budget may mean reducing staff numbers and the teaching unions are very concerned about possible redundancies.

How much money?

The first thing the governing body must do is find out exactly how much money it will be allocated by its LEA. When this is known it must be checked against the school roll to see whether the amount allocated according to the number and ages of the children is correct.

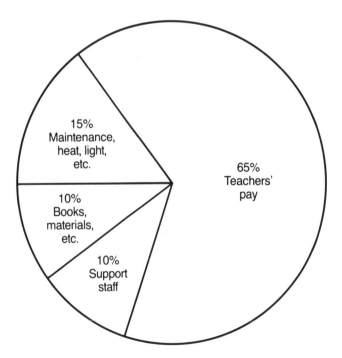

Fig. 17. Approximate use of a school's resources.

Where will the money go?
Bear in mind that most of the money allocated for your school will be for staffing—about 70–80 per cent of a school's budget (see Fig. 17).

Setting priorities
Before the governing body starts to worry about how to spend the money, it must decide on its priorities. There are several stages to go through.

1. Decide on the overall aims of the school, bearing in mind its need to provide the National Curriculum.
2. Decide what steps need to be taken to achieve these aims.
3. Decide what staff, equipment and other things are needed to take these steps, bearing in mind the LEA guidelines about contracts and its Health and Safety Policy.
4. Check that the amount of money allocated by the LEA is correct according to the numbers and ages of pupils in the school.
5. Decide which steps are the most important.
6. Decide for each step which items are most necessary.
7. Allow for fixed expenses and emergencies.
8. Divide the remainder of the money between the items needed for the various stages according to the order of priority.
9. Produce regular and accurate records of spending and income.

Questions to ask
Be as specific as possible:

• What kind of school are you aiming for?

• What should the school teach beyond the National Curriculum?

• How many teachers will you need?

• How many support staff, maintenance staff?

• What achievements are you aiming for?

• What out-of-school activities should the school provide?

• How will you work out whether the targets you are aiming for have been reached?

Planning for the future

The governing body should try to decide how to spend the money over several years. Long-term planning is better than short-term.

Setting the budget

When you have decided the school's priorities, you must work out what your **fixed costs** will be, for example:

- minimum staffing needs
- rent and rates
- headteacher's salary
- deputy headteacher's salary
- caretaker's salary
- heating
- lighting
- basic building maintenance

These are costs which stay the same (apart from inflation) from year to year. Of course, it may be possible to save on heating and lighting but governors should allow for a full amount and count any savings as a bonus.

Then you must allow for **emergencies**, such as falling rolls, meaning less pupils therefore less money, or unexpected damage to buildings by, for example, fire. You must also allow for providing supply teachers, if they become needed during the year.

Your school will have to provide a minimum level of **staffing** in order to supply the education demanded by law, but beyond this it is up to the governors to decide how many staff they employ and at what level. If two schools receive the same money from the formula but one school employs experienced teachers and the other mostly probationers, you can see that one school is going to have to pay extra from its budget if it wants to keep its experienced staff.

Analysing the budget

School **spending** will fall under approximately five headings:

- employee costs—teaching and non-teaching;
- costs concerning the buildings and grounds;
- running costs;
- miscellaneous expenses.

Income will come from:

- the amount allowed by the LEA;
- income the school creates, for example, by letting the premises.

BUDGET

Salary and wage costs	£
Teaching staff—permanent	1,453,000
—temporary	43,000
Support staff	57,000
Other non-teaching staff	135,000
Premises costs	
Maintenance—buildings	35,000
—grounds	6,000
Heating and lighting	54,000
Water	2,000
Rates	110,000
Supplies	
Books	7,000
Other equipment	44,000
Administration	
Printing and stationery	4,000
Photocopying and duplicating	7,000
Telephone	2,000
Other	4,000
Miscellaneous	
Staff training	5,000
	1,968,000
Income	
Delegated budget	1,963,000
Room hire	2,000
Fund raising	3,000
	1,968,000

Fig. 18. Model secondary school budget.

Asking the right questions

As you can see from the model secondary school budget in Fig. 18, several items can fall under each heading. Your job as a governor is to decide whether these costs are reasonable or whether a different costing would be more efficient. To do this you must ask questions to help you understand the budget.

For example, looking at the teaching costs, some questions could be:

- how many staff are there?

- what are their salaries?

- what is the size of each class?

- how many teachers have an incentive allowance?

- can any money be saved by not filling a vacancy for a term?

The governing body will have to make decisions about **staffing levels**. Maybe one school will pay for experienced staff but increase the pupil-teacher ratio, that is, how many pupils are taught by one teacher, in order to reduce the number of classes and therefore teachers. Another may decide to reduce the number of staff in order to reduce costs.

Similar kinds of questions can be asked under the other headings. You must make sure that you understand why money has been allocated in a certain way so that you can decide whether it is sensible.

Income

A school can raise money by letting school premises, fund-raising and other activities, obtaining donations, or selling items purchased with its allocated budget. Any income from such sources can be treated as an addition to the delegated budget.

LEAs must now have a policy on charging connected with the schools' delegated budgets. Governors can decide what charges to make as long as they keep within their budgets and do not charge for activities which the LEA has decided to pay for under its delegated budget scheme.

There are particular rules for letting to community groups or charging for certain school activities.

Charging for school activities
State schools cannot charge for admission to the school, nor for the education they provide during school hours. They can charge for individual music tuition. No charge can be made for any tuition given as part of a syllabus for a public exam.

Schools can charge for board and lodging on a residential trip. Any activity, such as a theatre trip, which takes place outside school hours can be charged for if it is not essential to a recognised course of study.

Regulations against charges do not stop the school asking for voluntary contributions from parents to help pay for activities. Not contributing must not affect whether a child takes part in any activity.

Income from letting of premises
County and maintained Special schools have control over the school premises outside school hours but under the direction of the LEA. If the school faces additional costs because of community activities, such as adult education classes, taking place on the premises then the LEA may compensate the school.

The LEA can direct the use of school premises in Voluntary controlled schools for weekends and aided schools for up to three days a week if the use is for young people.

Parent Staff Association funds
These are quite separate from school income and must be kept so. The governors and headteacher have no control over this money. If the PSA decides to make donations to the school fund this is entirely up to its members. The PSA will have to arrange for its own accounts to be banked and audited.

AFTER THE BUDGET

What happens once the governing body has decided how to spend the money and has issued its budget statement at the beginning of the financial year? Can governors now relax?

Amendments

The governing body has the freedom to decide how to spend the money it has been allocated. That means that if there is a reason to alter the way the money is spent during the year, this can be done.

Schools can save on one area of spending and use the money saved for another area (virement). It is normally possible to hold unused money over until the next year, but it is worth checking what the position is with your LEA.

The LEA may decide that it has saved money for you by, for example, putting in more efficient windows and so reducing heat and light bills. In that case it may decide to reduce next year's budget for the school on the grounds that the school is getting its savings in the form of reduced energy bills.

If money is needed during the year, for example, to pay for repairs or supply teachers, then this can be done by making savings elsewhere. This will mean changing the details of the original budget. (Unless the LEA makes more money available, it will not be possible to increase the total.)

In order to make sure that such changes can be made, the governors must be kept up to date on the way the money is being spent.

Monitoring

Regular financial reports from the headteacher or subcommittee of governors are vital. Only by careful monitoring of the spending and income of the school during the course of the financial year can decisions be made about whether to depart from the original budget and transfer money to another use.

Careful watch needs to be kept on how the money is spent in case it is spent too quickly or slowly.

Governors are accountable to the parents, community and LEA for how the money is managed and so must keep careful watch on it.

Where to go for help

Your LEA will provide help and advice to the governors about LMS schemes and how to operate them and it is always possible to ask your LEA for advice. It will provide advice and professional help with such things as contracts, staffing and building maintenance as well as doing the calculations for National Insurance and Superannuation contributions.

For most of the time, however, it is up to the governors themselves to make sense of the money.

What do you do if none of the governors feels able to discuss a budget or work out a budget with the headteacher? Your governing body may decide that it is useful to **co-opt** someone from the business community who is knowledgeable about finance to help. The Institute of Chartered Accountants in England and Wales (ICAEW), for example, has district societies and local branches which may be able to suggest Chartered Accountants who would like to help your governing body as co-opted members.

A parent who is not an elected parent governor but who has financial expertise may be willing to be co-opted on the governing body.

All governors should, of course, take any available opportunity to go on governor **training courses** about finance for governors.

The headteacher may be an expert in handling school money, in which case delegation to him or her may be sensible. But note what I have said about speaking up if you are not happy about how some of the money is to be spent. If you don't know what an item on the budget means, ask.

If the headteacher is not happy about organising the money then the same options for help apply.

CHECKLIST

1. Take an interest in the money. Governors have a responsibility for spending it.

2. When looking at a budget statement, look for the numbers which tell you how much money the school is allowed and how much has been spent.

3. If you don't understand an item in a budget statement, ask.

4. Don't be afraid to challenge spending on certain items if you disagree with it.

5. Find out what your school's LMS scheme is and ask for it to be explained to all the governors.

6. Find out whether your governing body has a clear management plan. Are the aims and objectives clear?

7. Has the budget been planned for more than one year?

8. Take every chance to go on training course for governors about financial management.

9. Has your school worked out a basic budget for the next financial year?

10. Does your governing body have a governor who understands finance? If not, suggest co-opting one.

9
The Curriculum

The word 'curriculum' has traditionally been used to separate 'them' from 'us', that is, the teachers from the public. It is a word that throws people into a panic because they assume it is something that only the teachers as experts can understand. Even governors have been known to decline to discuss the curriculum with teachers because 'the staff know best'.

The governors have an important part to play in overseeing what will be taught in schools. They now have control over the secular curriculum, which is everything which is taught in school except religious education. To be effective as a governor you must not be afraid of the word, nor of voicing your opinion about the curriculum.

What is the curriculum?

The word simply means a course—in schools, a course of study. It is simply what the children are taught in schools. According to the Education Reform Act 1988 (ERA), it consists of the activities which are taught which promote 'the spiritual, moral, cultural, mental and physical development of pupils at the school' and prepares them for 'the opportunities, responsibilities and experiences of adult life'.

Do not forget that there is also a 'hidden curriculum'. This is the attitudes, values and prejudices which children absorb at school. So what a child is taught includes this 'hidden curriculum'.

All this sounds fine, but do we know what is being taught? Up until the 1988 Act, the answer for most people was 'I'm not sure'. The public knew that children were taught reading, writing and mathematics but were hazy about what other subjects were available.

In fact, because of lack of teachers' expertise in some subjects or the need to limit teaching to subjects required for exams, some children left primary school without a good knowledge of maths or science, or secondary school without more than a dabbling in a foreign language.

All this has now changed with the advent of the ERA which has brought in the National Curriculum. Whatever one thinks of the National Curriculum, it is here to stay. It is the job of the governors to ensure that it is put into practice in the best way possible.

THE NATIONAL CURRICULUM

The National Curriculum is a group of subjects which all children in England and Wales between the ages of five and fourteen must be taught. Pupils can drop some subjects for the fourteen to sixteen stage. Each subject has a series of stages which pupils go through to reach approved standards. There are regular ages for being assessed and parents will be fully informed of their child's progress.

Which subjects?

Everyone now knows what subjects are being taught because they will be the same in all maintained schools in England and Wales. (Although schools in the private sector do not have to follow the National Curriculum, many will do so.)

Parents need not worry that their children will be deprived of the three 'Rs', reading, writing and arithmetic. These have an important place in the National Curriculum.

There are ten **Foundation subjects** taught:

* English
* Mathematics
* Science
* Technology
* History
* Geography
* Music
* Art
* Physical Education (PE)
* A modern foreign language

Of these subjects, three are called **Core subjects**:

* English
* Mathematics
* Science

Note : In Wales (in Welsh-speaking schools) Welsh will be a Core subject and English one of the other Foundation subjects. In English-speaking schools in Wales, Welsh will be a Foundation subject but will not be compulsory after the age of 14.

How much of the timetable will be National Curriculum?

From September 1995 80 per cent of the timetable will be used for teaching the National Curriculum leaving the equivalent of a day a week to be used at a school's discretion. 14–16 year olds will have a reduced National Curriculum timetable of 60% leaving schools free to introduce vocational courses or alternative academic options. The reductions will be made in Foundation subjects. There will be a reduction in foreign language teaching from 11 years old.

Core subjects

The three Core subjects, English, Mathematics and Science, are seen as the backbone of the Curriculum. Teaching the National Curriculum in schools should ensure that each child leaves school with a good grounding in these subjects. The days of the scientist who has hardly read a book or the Art student who knows nothing about mathematics should be past.

However, because these subjects will be taught from the age of five, the country will need a greater number of teachers qualified to teach science and mathematics. Part of the governors' job, therefore, will be to ensure that teachers in such subjects are employed in their school. (See Chapter 7 on appointing staff.)

Foundation subjects

The other Foundation subjects will probably be taught in an integrated way. We best know this by the topic work of primary school age. This is a way of children learning many skills and subjects by studying one topic. For example, a study of the local park could include reading, writing, art, science (nature study), geography (the park in relation to the local area) and maths (measuring the height of trees). Because the amount of time available to teach all the subjects will be limited, this is probably the way that the Foundation subjects will be taught at secondary level too, although they can also be taught as single subjects at that level.

How old will the children be?

All the subjects, except a foreign language, will be taught to all children from the age of five to the age of fourteen. A modern foreign language will be taught at secondary level. Pupils will be able to drop art, music and history or geography at fourteen. How much PE will be required remains uncertain.

How does it work?

Each subject is divided into **Attainment Targets**. Each of these Attainment Targets is a group of learning skills and facts which children need to understand a subject. There are different numbers of Attainment Targets in each subject.

Each Attainment Target has ten **Levels of Attainment**. These are the stages children have to go through as they learn the subject. At each level there are specific skills or facts a child must know before he or she can be said to have reached that level.

The idea is that children should not be graded as better or worse than their friends of the same age, but they will be assessed individually to see whether they possess the skills and knowledge needed for each level.

The Attainment Targets are divided into groups, or **Profiles**, so that it is easier for the teacher and parent to understand what the child is doing. For example, the Writing Profile of the English curriculum consists of the Attainment Targets concerned with Spelling, Handwriting and Constructing and Conveying Meaning.

Assessment

Children will be assessed at regular intervals. These will not be tests as we understand them, but activities designed to find out what level each child is at in each Attainment Target for each subject. They are not meant to grade children but should be used to find out what the child knows and what help he or she needs in order to progress. The teacher can use these assessments to plan the next stage of work for each child.

The assessments are made by **Standard Assessment Tasks** (**SATs**), which are designed to find out:

• how well a child understands and interprets instructions.

• how far they get with the task that is set.

• what the result looks like.

These activities are designed to seem as much like ordinary classwork as possible so that the children do not realise they are being assessed.

In primary school, several subjects will be assessed together in SATs, but in secondary school some will be assessed separately.

Because the SATs will involve a series of tasks, children may take several days or several weeks to do them.

The tasks will involve all kinds of recording besides writing, such as drawing, computers and painting. The children will be given the chance to work and discuss the tasks with other children. This is part of the assessment. At other times they will work on their own.

SATs are only part of the assessment procedure. Besides these, teachers will be continually assessing each child and will make their own report on the child at the assessment stages.

When will children be assessed?
Children will be assessed at **Key Reporting Stages** in their school career, *ie* the ages of seven, eleven, fourteen and sixteen.

Children will only be assessed on the three core subjects. Teachers will make their own assessments of pupils' attainment levels in the other foundation subjects at these ages.

Controversy over testing led to a widespread boycott of tests for 14 year olds in 1993. The government hopes that tests will continue now that there is to be a reduced National Curriculum and testing of Foundation subjects has been postponed. At sixteen pupils take GCSE exams.

Information for parents
When the National Curriculum is working properly each parent will receive a **Programme of Study** for the year stating what work the class will be doing. The parent will also receive details of the teacher's scheme of work for the child stating which Attainment Targets the child will be trying to do and at what levels.

If any assessments take place during the year the parent will receive details of these and the results of the assessments for each Profile.

There will also be information given so that parents can compare their child's progress with the class as a whole. The general results for each class will be compared to the school as a whole.

Role of governors
Governors must ensure that the school has the teachers and resources to provide the National Curriculum and that all pupils entitled to it receive it.

CHILDREN WITH SPECIAL NEEDS

Some of the children in your school may have learning difficulties. This means that they have great difficulty in learning as well as other children of their age or that they have a disability which stops them taking part in the education provided by their LEA.

Some of these children whose learning difficulties are particularly severe are given a '**Statement of Special Needs**' after experts, the headteacher and parents have discussed the case. This is a written statement of their learning problem and sets out what is needed to help the child get the best education possible.

Children can be taught in Special schools or units attached to the main school. Other children with learning difficulties but whose problems are not so severe can be taught in the mainstream of the school.

The trend now is to **integrate** statemented children into mainstream schooling. This can cause a lot of problems which the governors will have to give consideration to.

Children with special needs are entitled to the full range of the National Curriculum and every effort should be made to make sure that they receive it.

Role of governors

Governors have a duty to ensure that the LEA and the school meets the needs of these children. Extra staff might be needed with a duty to look after the children: extra equipment and resources might also be required. The school building may need to be modified to allow access for children with physical difficulties. Children with special needs must be able to take part in as much of the National Curriculum as possible.

The government's aim is to encourage children who have a 'statement of Special Needs' to take part in the full range of the National Curriculum as much as possible. However, if the headteacher feels that a certain child would benefit by missing part of the curriculum or by having it modified in some way, she or he can do so as long as the parents, governing body and the LEA are informed (see Fig. 19).

---

18. The special education provision for any pupil specified in a statement under section 7 of the 1981 Act of his special educational needs may include provision—

    (a) excluding the application of the provisions of the National Curriculum; or

    (b) applying those provisions with such modifications as may be specified in the statement.

Fig. 19. National Curriculum and Special Needs—Education Reform Act 1988. (With acknowledgement to the Controller of Her Majesty's Stationery Office.)

If the parents disagree with this, they can appeal to the governing body which must either support the headteacher's decision or ask for it to be changed. If the parents are still not satisfied they can appeal to the LEA.

ROLE OF HEADTEACHER AND GOVERNORS

The headteacher's role

The headteacher's responsibility is to provide for the 'determination and organisation of the secular curriculum' in the school and to make sure that it is followed (EA 86). The secular curriculum is everything to be taught except religious education (RE—see below). The headteacher must take into account the LEA statement about the curriculum and also the governors' statement which might modify what the LEA has said.

Account must also be taken of what people in the community think and what the local chief of police has to say about curriculum matters which might be connected with the police.

What this means for the governor is that the headteacher decides what is to be taught and how, as long as it is in line with what the LEA and the governing body says about the National Curriculum.

The governors' role

Governors now have a much more active part to play in what is taught in schools. The LEA must issue a statement to all head-teachers and governing bodies about what it feels should be done about the curriculum, bearing in mind that it has to make sure that the National Curriculum is brought in.

The governing body of each school must consider what the aim of this statement is and must then decide whether it needs to be modified for their school.

Now that most governing bodies will have financial responsibility for staff as well as buildings and equipment they will have an important role to play in providing the school with the right teachers and equipment to enable it to implement the National Curriculum.

RELIGIOUS EDUCATION

This is not one of the Foundation subjects but is also mentioned in the 1988 ERA as part of the National Curriculum.

Act of worship

Every pupil in a maintained school must take part in a daily religious act of worship either entirely or for the most part broadly Christian (see Fig. 20). This can either be in a whole school assembly or in smaller groups.

Parents have the right to withdraw their children from this assembly. Controlled schools can take account of any rules laid down for religious worship in the school's trust deeds. Special schools must make provision for all pupils to attend RE and religious worship as far as is practicable.

Where the school has many pupils from a different faith the school can ask for permission from the Standing Advisory Council on Religious Education (SACRE) which every LEA must set up. If the Council decides that a Christian assembly is not appropriate it can give permission for worship to be broadly of another faith.

Religious education

6.—(1) Subject to section 9 of this Act, all pupils in attendance at a maintained school shall on each school day take part in an act of collective worship.

(2) The arrangements for the collective worship in a school required by this section may, in respect of each school day, provide for a single act of worship for all pupils or for separate acts of worship for pupils in different age groups or in different school groups.

Special provisions as to collective worship in county schools

7.—(1) Subject to the following provisions of this section, in the case of a county school the collective worship required in the school by section 6 of this Act shall be wholly or mainly of a broadly Christian character.

(2) For the purposes of subsection (1) above, collective worship is of a broadly Christian character if it reflects the broad traditions of Christian belief without being distinctive of any particular Christian denomination.

Fig. 20. Religious education and collective worship—Education Reform Act 1988. (With acknowledgement to the Controller of Her Majesty's Stationery Office.)

Problems

This part of the Reform Act is already causing conflict because parents of different faiths expect different things from the school's RE provision.

The governors, with the headteacher and the LEA, have a duty to make sure that religious education is provided in school according to the ERA, but they must be aware of potential causes of conflict.

Many schools will probably do what they have always done and that is to make the broadly Christian element of religious education the caring attitudes which strike a chord in all the major religions.

SEX EDUCATION

Governors have a duty to decide whether sex education should be taught in their school. If they decide that it should be taught, then the teaching must 'encourage pupils to have due regard to moral considerations and the value of family life' (see Fig. 21).

18.—(2) The articles of government for every such school shall provide for it to be the duty of the governing body—

(a) to consider separately (while having due regard to the local authority's statement under section 17 of this Act) the question whether sex education should form part of the secular curriculum for the school; and

(b) to make, and keep up to date, a separate written statement—

(i) of their policy with regard to the content and organisation of the relevant part of the curriculum; or

(ii) where they conclude that sex education should not form part of the secular curriculum, of that conclusion.

46. The local education authority by whom any county, voluntary or special school is maintained, and the governing body and head teacher of the school, shall take such steps as are reasonably practicable to secure that where sex education is given to any registered pupils at the school it is given in such a manner as to have due regard to moral considerations and the value of family life.

Fig. 21. Sex education—Education (No. 2) Act 1986.
(With acknowledgement to the Controller of Her Majesty's Stationery Office.)

When they have made a decision the governors must put this decision in writing. If sex education will be taught, governors must draw up a written statement of their policy about the content and organisation of this subject in their school and keep it up to date.

Although the government and LEAs want to encourage schools to teach sex education, much will depend on the willingness and ability of the staff to do so. Governors will therefore expect to be involved in discussions with the headteacher and probably the staff about this. They will also want to take into account the views of the parents. (The views of parent governors will be particularly useful in finding out what the feelings of parents are about this.)

Legal requirements about sex education do not apply to aided and special schools but they may consider adopting similar arrangements.

POLITICAL EDUCATION

The EA 86 made it clear that teaching should not be politically biased. In other words, teachers must give balanced views when they touch on politics. Children in primary school must not take part in party political activities within the school or elsewhere organised by a member of staff acting as such. (See Fig. 22.)

44.—(1) The local education authority by whom any county, voluntary or special school is maintained, and the governing body and head teacher of the school shall forbid—

(a) the pursuit of partisan political activities by any of those registered pupils at the school who are junior pupils; and

(b) the promotion of any partisan political views in the teaching of any subject in the school.

(2) In the case of activities which take place otherwise than on the premises of the school concerned, subsection (1)(a) above applies only where arrangements for junior pupils to take part in the activities are made by any member of the staff of the school (in his capacity as such) or by anyone acting on his, or the school's behalf.

Fig. 22. Political indoctrination—Education (No. 2) Act 1986.
(With acknowledgement to the Controller of Her Majesty's Stationery Office.)

The governors, as well as the headteacher and the LEA, have a duty to ensure that this is what is happening. Most teachers are going to be very careful about not politically indoctrinating children but governors should be aware of this rule.

WELSH MEDIUM EDUCATION

In Wales there are two main languages, Welsh and English. The importance of retaining Welsh as a language is recognised by the government.

Whether the curriculum is taught largely in Welsh or English depends on whether the school is in a mainly Welsh or English speaking part of Wales.

Where one of the two languages is the main language spoken then the other language must be taught as well. Now that the National Curriculum is in operation the main language will be a core subject and the other a foundation subject. From September 1995 Welsh as a second language in English-speaking schools will not be compulsory for 14–16 year olds.

CHECKLIST

1. Don't be afraid of the word 'curriculum'.

2. Find out how your school is coping with teaching the National Curriculum.

3. Find out what your school needs to teach the National Curriculum effectively—more staff? specialised staff? different equipment? building alterations?

4. Have you found out how your school caters for children with special needs?

5. What arrangements has the school made for religious education?

6. Has the governing body decided whether sex education should be taught in the school?

7. Have the governors made sure that the staff are aware that teaching must not be politically biased?

8. In Wales, is your school providing Welsh and English as a core or foundation subject as necessary?

10
Governors and Parents

The relationship between governors and parents is extremely important. The governors' job is to make sure that the school provides the kind of education for the pupils in the school that the parents want and expect, within the limits of the rules and regulations of the government and the LEA. It is therefore very important that governors find out what the views of the parents are on as many issues as possible which affect the school.

IMPORTANCE OF MEETING PARENTS

What sort of things can the parents tell a governor and why is it important to get to know parents and what their views are?

Parents know their own children best, but they also have contact with and observe other children at close quarters. They know, for example, whether their child and others are bored in the classroom, whether they think the discipline is adequate, whether the headteacher is giving them enough information and the sort of information they want, whether their child and others experience the results of sexism or racism or are bullied at school, whether they consider the standard of education high enough.

Parents have **views** on uniform, buildings, equipment, afterschool care, playground supervision, subject choices allowed for GSCEs, school trips and a host of other items connected with school life. To ignore their views is to ignore the people most directly affecting the children's lives.

Parents also have **much to offer the school**. Perhaps some can translate for teachers or translate school letters, help with sewing, cooking or reading, give a talk, for example, on computing or genealogy, accompany teachers and children on school trips, know someone who wants to be a school dinner supervisor, or simply provide lots of cardboard for a depleted stock cupboard.

Governors should make the effort to get out and meet parents. Parent governors may find this easier than other governors because

Model Constitution

Please note this is a Model Constitution. It may be varied to suit particular circumstances in each Association. However, it is important to note Clauses 2, 24 and 25. The wording of these clauses has been agreed with the Charity Commission and the Inland Revenue so that inclusion in their entirety establishes an association as a charity for tax purposes.

Model

1. The name of the Association shall be . . . .
   . . . .
2. **The object of the Association is to advance the education of the pupils in the school. In furtherance of this object the Association may:**
   (a) **Develop more extended relationships between the staff, parents and others associated with the school.**
   (b) **Engage in activities which support the school and advance the education of the pupils attending it.**
   (c) **Provide and assist in the provision of facilities for education at the school (not normally provided by the local Education Authority).**
3. The Association shall be non-party political and non-sectarian.
4. The Association shall take out Public Liability and Personal Accident Insurance to cover its meetings, activities, Officers and Committee. (Note 1)
5. The Association may appoint a President.
6. The names of the Vice Presidents shall be submitted at the Annual General Meeting. (These are usually people the Association wishes to honour.)
7. Membership shall consist of all parents and/or guardians of pupils attending the school and all Teachers. (Note 2)
8. The management of the Association shall be vested in a Committee consisting of the following Officers:
   Chairman, Vice Chairman, Honorary Secretary, Honorary Treasurer together with (. . .) other members. (Note 3)
9. The Officers and Committee shall be elected at the Annual General Meeting and shall serve until the commencement of the next Annual General Meeting.
10. (. . .) members of the Committee shall constitute a quorum. (Note 4)
11. The Committee shall have the power to co-opt a maximum of (. . .). (Note 5)
12. The Committee may appoint sub-committees, as it deems necessary and shall prescribe their function provided that all acts and proceedings of any such sub-committee shall be reported to the Committee as soon as possible and provided further that no such sub-committee shall expend funds of the Association otherwise than in accordance with a budget agreed by the Committee.
13. Committee meetings shall be held at least once each term.
14. The Annual General Meeting will be held on (. . .). (Note 6). At the Annual General Meeting, the chair shall be taken by the Chairman or in his/her absence the Vice Chairman of the Committee.
15. Nominations shall be proposed and seconded by members and should have the consent of the nominee. Nominations may be made at any time prior to the commencement of the Annual General Meeting.
16. The Committee may fill casual vacancies by co-option until the next Annual General Meeting.
17. Two Auditors who are not members of the Committee shall be elected annually at the AGM to audit the accounts and books of the Association.
18. Special General Meetings may be called at the written request of a minimum of 10 members.
19. Thirty days notice shall be given of any Special General Meeting to all members of the Association.

20. The Honorary Treasurer shall be responsible for keeping account of all Income and Expenditure and shall present a Financial report to all Committee meetings, and shall present the accounts duly audited for approval by the members at the Annual General Meeting.

21. Bank Accounts shall be operated in the name of the Association and withdrawals shall be made on the signature of any two of the Officers of the Association.

22. The financial year shall commence on (. . .) (Note 7)

23. Any matter not provided for in the Constitution and concerning the organisation and activities of the Association shall be dealt with by the Committee whose decision shall be final.

24. **No alteration to this Constitution may be made except at the Annual General Meeting or a Special General Meeting called for this purpose. No amendments or alterations shall be made without the prior written permission of The Charity Commission to Clauses 2, 24 and 25 and no alteration shall be made which could cause the Association to cease to be a charity in law. Alterations to the Constitution shall receive the assent of two thirds of the members present and voting at an AGM or Special General Meeting.**

25. **The Association may be dissolved by a resolution presented at a Special General Meeting called for this purpose. The resolution must have the assent of two thirds of those present and voting. Such resolution may give instructions for the disposal of any assets remaining after satisfying any outstanding debts and liabilities. These assets shall not be distributed among the members of the Association but will be given to the school for the benefit of the children of the school, or in the event of a school closure to the school to which the majority of children of the closing school will go, in any manner which is exclusively charitable in law. If effect cannot be given to this provision then the assets can be given to some other charitable purpose.**

Notes

1. Membership of the National Confederation of Parent Teacher Associations automatically provides this.

2. Membership can also include Past Parents, Grandparents, Friends of the School, Ancillary Staff and Governors.

3. The size of the Committee should depend upon the number of children on roll. A small school might have a Committee of Five plus Officers, 1 large one, Twelve plus Officers.
   The Headteacher may be a member of the Committee.

4. A quorum would depend on the size of the whole Committee, it must be a third of the members. **Minimum three.**

5. Co-opted members. The number would depend on the size of the Committee, usually two co-optees would be sufficient. They could have voting rights.

6. The AGM should preferably take place during the Autumn Term to enable new parents to be involved from the start of the new School year.

7. The financial year will be for twelve months.

Fig. 23. Model PTA constitution. (With acknowledgement to NCPTA.)

they are more likely to be around when other parents are, but all governors should try to do so if they are to have a rounded picture of the school community.

PARENT STAFF ASSOCIATIONS

I use the term Parent Staff Association to include the many forms of association run largely by parents to communicate with and help the school.

Some are the traditional Parent Teacher Associations (PTAs) which include parents and teachers and have a formal **constitution**. They are under the umbrella of the National Confederation of Parent Teachers Associations which gives guidance and support (see Fig. 23). A more up-to-date name is Parent Staff Association in recognition of the importance of support staff such as dinner ladies and other helpers in the running of the school.

Other organisations work under the name of Friends of the School or similar names. These are usually more informal groups. Some headteachers prefer groups like this because the term PTA conjures up a powerful organisation with formal authority in conflict with the headteacher. In fact any organisation is as powerful and influential as its members make it.

All these groups are forums where parents, staff, governors and any other people invited by the group can come to discuss what goes on in the school and how best to support it. Sometimes speakers are invited to talk about aspects of the curriculum or the staff might be invited to provide a display.

Fundraising

Fundraising is often a large part of a PSA's activity because of shortage of money for equipment or buildings. This is often derided as not being the job of a PSA which should have more important things to do. In fact, apart from the obvious need in many cases to provide extra income for the school, a fundraising event is often one of the few occasions when parents will come into school.

For example, in my school parents were reluctant to come into the school for talks, meetings or displays, but cake sales used to see the hall packed! Parents were happy not only to bake cakes but to come in great numbers and buy other people's offerings and eat them while having a cup of tea. Not only was a lot of money raised easily, but the parents, staff and governors had a chance to meet and talk informally.

Purpose of PSAs

Each group will have its own priorities and way of doing things, but the main purpose of all is to exchange ideas and information and determine courses of action which might benefit the school. The groups provide the chance for a working partnership between all the adults concerned with the children's education.

Governors and PSAs

As a governor you should try to get to these meetings occasionally. Not only will this show your willingness to hear what parents have to say about different issues but it will give parents a chance to discuss their ideas about the school with a governor who can then go back to the next governors meeting more informed. (See Fig. 24.)

Report to Marydale School Parent Staff Association from Michael Jones (parent governor)

I attended the governors meeting which took place on 14th May in the school hall. Of the four parent governors, only myself and Cathy Barnes were present. Peter Black did send his apologies—he had flu.

The main business of the meeting was a discussion of the staffing problems facing the school and the various ways of tackling this. I put forward the view of the PSA that we should collect a petition and present it via the governing body to our MP and the Chief Education Officer. This was agreed.

A special meeting is to be held to discuss whether sex education should be taught in the school. I am on the subcommittee to draft a report to the meeting so I shall be asking the views of the parents present.

After a long campaign the governors have persuaded the LEA to mend the roof, and the swing doors are to be renewed next term.

I informed the governing body of the parents' concern about car parking in the school gateway and the headteacher has agreed to ask our home beat officer to be present at the end of the school day for a while to deter drivers.

Fig. 24. Model report from parent governor to PSA.

OTHER MEETING PLACES

PSA meetings are not the only places where parents and governors can meet. There are many chances in any school for informal contact which at the same time shows to parents, staff and children that governors support the work of the school. On some occasions a governor might be the only person present if parents have been unable to attend, so it is important to children that adults other than staff see their efforts and appreciate them.

Special events

Opportunities to visit the school or participate in events might include:

- plays;

- concerts;

- social events such as dances, discos, wine and cheese parties;

- multi-cultural evenings;

- sports days;

- special assemblies for such occasions as Chinese New Year, Christmas and Ramadan, or for classes to show work;

- displays of work for such things as school trips, topic work, special projects or a particular section of the curriculum;

- fundraising events such as fairs, fetes, sales.

Not every governor can get to all such events, but if you attempt to get to one or two during the term you will get a much better idea of what the school is doing.

Once parents get to know your face you will find that they will come and talk to you before, after or during these events.

The playground

You can also meet parents in the school playground. Parent governors will obviously have more opportunity to do this because they may, if their child is in primary school, take or collect their child from school and know some of the other parents or have got to know other parents through their children's friends. Parent governors who work will have to find the time in other ways, either by asking for time off work to attend an important school event or by attending evening socials.

Every governor who can be at the school at the beginning and end of the day can go into a school playground and talk to parents. It might take a bit of nerve to introduce yourself with 'Hello, I'm Mr Jones, one of the school governors. I'm trying to get to know some of the parents. How does your child like the school?' but it can be done. If you are nervous why not get someone you know to introduce you to a few parents?

Not all governors will have the free time to do this, but for those who can the playground is an excellent meeting place.

REPRESENTING PARENTS' VIEWS

Parents can ask any governor to help with their problem or to put their views to the governing body. They do not have to confine themselves to talking to the parent governors, although many will choose to do so.

If a parent wants to tell you his or her views you should listen. For example, a parent may feel that her child is being continually bullied because discipline in the school is lax. If that parent wants you to make known those views to the governing body you have several courses open to you:

1. You could **refuse** to do so. You are perfectly entitled to refuse to put any views to the governing body, other than your own. However, any governing body which does not listen to the views of the parents cannot be said to be fully representative or accountable to the community it serves. I'm sure you will want to make sure that the parents' views are heard.

2. You could put forward the **view of the individual**. If you do this you should make it clear that you are expressing someone else's viewpoint at their request.

3. A more sensible approach would be to talk to as many parents as possible to find out what the majority think and then put these views to other governors as **minority and majority viewpoints** as far as you have been able to discover them.

4. If you think that an issue is important enough to need the views of all the parents, you could ask the governors to arrange with the

school for a **questionnaire** to be sent home with each child. You will not get a reply from every parent, but you should get enough to let the governors know what the majority of parents think.

5. **Your own view** may be completely different from any of these and you can make this known as well. The governors then have a basis for discussion with knowledge of the various ideas expressed.

Problems

If an individual parent is not just expressing a view but has a specific problem your response will depend on the nature of the problem. Mrs White may be concerned that her child is being picked on by a particular teacher. Your response to this will depend on whether she has spoken to the teacher and the headteacher and what she thinks she wants done about the problem.

Questions you need to ask could be:

1. Why do you think this is happening?
2. Have you spoken to the teacher?
3. What was the teacher's response?
4. Have you spoken to the headteacher?
5. What do you want the school to do?

Your response might be to approach the headteacher and then arrange a meeting between him or her and the parent, perhaps with you present.

First of all you must **listen** to the parent carefully. Not all parents are equally good at expressing what they mean and you should make sure that you have fully understood what the problem is.

Sometimes all that is needed is reassurance about some aspect of school life. If so and you understand the aspect then all that might be needed is an explanation of the process and assurance about any measures that are being taken.

Complaints about teaching

If a parent wants to complain about the teaching their child is receiving you should encourage them to talk first of all to the teacher or, if that is not possible, to the headteacher. Some parents find talking to teachers or headteachers frightening and become defensive or aggressive. You could offer to arrange a meeting and perhaps stay with the parent while it is taking place, not to take part but to accompany and reassure the parent.

Official procedures

In some cases there are official procedures to go through; for example, if a pupil is to be excluded from school. In that case it is not your job to decide what happens, but to explain to the parent what his or her rights are and what has to be done. It is then up to the headteacher and others to make sure that the procedures are carried out correctly. This might involve the governing body of which you are a part. It is at that point you will get a chance to express your views on the problem.

Ask for help

If a parent comes to you with a difficult problem or a problem about which you are unsure how to help, then you must ask for help from the headteacher or chairman about how to proceed. There is no shame in asking for help. You are not an expert and any parent is entitled to the best help possible with any problem concerning their children.

Your privacy

In a rare case you may get pestered at home by a parent continually telephoning or calling at your home. If this happens once you can see it as part of the job. If it happens enough to disrupt your life or if you are threatened in any way, then you should contact the headteacher and the chairman of the governors. If the situation cannot be sorted out by help and discussion with the parent then you should contact the police. You are entitled to your safety and privacy as much as any other citizen.

THE ROLE OF THE PARENT GOVERNOR

There is often a lot of confusion among parents and other governors about the role of the parent governors. Governors tend to regard them as the only people capable of reporting parents' views, indeed they sometimes seem to think that that is their only role.

Parents, on the other hand, are inclined to regard parent governors as people who can be ordered to vote in particular ways and to turn up to any parent meetings.

•
Representative parent

You must be quite clear that a parent governor is not a representative of the parents. He or she is a representative parent. Just as when we elect a councillor or MP, we trust them to act in our best interests, so a parent governor is elected in trust to do the same thing for the school. Other governors who are not parent governors may also be parents with children at the school.

A parent governor cannot be ordered (mandated) to vote in a particular way at the request of the parents, nor to turn up to meetings and report at the parents' orders. He or she can, like the other governors, make up his or her own mind about the issues discussed and vote in the way he or she considers best for the school.

Attendance at parents meetings

I have been at PSA meetings where some parents have got quite angry when a parent governor who had made the effort to turn up, declined to be ordered to turn up at yet another meeting and give a full report about something to the group. As a conscientious governor, her time was already stretched. She attended as many PSA meetings as she could and could not attend any more.

This shows a typical misunderstanding of the parent governor's role. Because parent governors are more likely to know many of their fellow parents and have easier access to them it is expected that they can be ordered about by them. Not so.

Availability

A good parent governor will want to be available to parents as much as possible and to make their views known to the governing body, but indeed so will any governor. Parents are entitled to talk to any governor; parent governors are just easier to get at.

Views and votes

A parent governor who is asked the views of the parents should say so if he or she doesn't know, or if the views are not his or her own. How that person votes is his or her own decision after hearing the facts.

Being a parent governor does not stop you expressing views on anything on which other governors do, nor does it stop other governors expressing views about the parents.

Reports on school events

Parent governors are more likely to be at school events and meetings not attended by other governors, and they could, as a courtesy, give a report to other governors although they cannot be ordered to do so.

The press

A governor might be approached by the press to comment on a situation at the school. It is not an individual governor's place to comment in this way. A governor may not have a full overall knowledge of the situation. A parent governor in particular would have to be careful about not expressing a view which might be misinterpreted as one which is held by the parents as a whole.

The correct procedure in this case, indeed for any governor so approached, is to decline to comment and refer the reporter to the chairman of the governors or the clerk to the governors. The chairman can speak on behalf of the governing body as a whole, but he too should not comment to the press until he has checked with the clerk that it is sensible for him to do so.

The reason for this way of reacting to press enquiries is so that the correct facts are presented and nothing is said in public which might inflame a tricky situation.

Acting on behalf of governors

No individual governor can act on behalf of the governors unless he or she has been asked to do so.

ANNUAL REPORT TO PARENTS

One of the most important jobs of the governing body is to report to the parents once a year about what has been happening in the school and about how the governors, headteacher and LEA have carried out their duties in respect of the school.

The report is often written by the headteacher with the help of a subcommittee of governors. The headteacher obviously knows best what the school has achieved over the previous year, but the report is officially from the governors so they must decide what goes in it.

As a governor you might be asked to sit on the subcommittee to help draft the report. In any case you and the other governors will need to read and amend or approve the report at a full governors meeting.

The report has to be followed by a meeting for all the parents.

Contents

The written report to the parents should be brief but contain everything necessary so that the parents get full information about the school. The Education (No.2) Act 1986 has laid down the minimum information it should contain:

- details of the date, time, place and agenda of the Annual Parents Meeting;

- a statement saying that the purpose of the meeting is to discuss the governors' report to the parents and how well the governors, headteacher and LEA have carried out their duties to the school;

- a report on the results of any resolutions passed at the previous meeting;

- name of each governor, what kind of governor, who appointed them, and when their term of office ends;

- name and address of the chairman and clerk to the governors;

- arrangements for the next parent governors election;

- financial statement summarising the latest LEA statement, saying how any sum available to the governors was used and whether any gifts were made to the school;

- details of any public exams (in secondary schools);

- how the governing body is trying to strengthen links with the community and police;

- notice of any information which the governing body has made available about such things as syllabuses.

As you can see there is a lot of detail required, but many schools will want to add more information than this.

Language of report

The governors can produce the report in other languages in addition to English, if they think it necessary, and they must produce it in any languages which the LEA orders.

This is all very well and governing bodies would like to do this, but unless their LEA can provide a speedy translation service or the school has parents willing and able to translate the document, this remains for many schools an unattainable ideal.

Getting the report to parents

The governors must try as hard as possible to make sure that all parents get a (free) copy of the report and that copies are made available for anyone to look at in the school. The report should get to parents at least two weeks before the meeting.

Annual Parents Meeting

The Annual Parents Meeting is a very important opportunity for parents and governors to discuss the progress of the school and for parents to question the governors', headteacher's and LEA's efforts on the school's behalf. Some schools get a packed meeting for this; at others only a handful of parents turn up. Apart from apathy it may be that parents see no need to attend a meeting when they have a written report to hand.

Those entitled to attend the meeting include all parents of children registered at the school, the headteacher, the governing body and anyone invited by the governing body. Only the parents of registered pupils can vote. Resolutions can only be passed by the meeting if the number of parents equals 20 per cent of the number of pupils. So the **quorum** for a school of three hundred pupils would be sixty.

The governing body must run the meeting, which means in practice that it will be under the control of the chairman of the governors. The governing body must consider any resolutions the parents pass which are their concern, as must the headteacher and the LEA. If the headteacher is sent a resolution from the meeting he or she must comment on it in writing for the next governors' report. Ideally, of course, resolutions should be acted upon as soon as possible and the parents informed of the result well before the next Annual Parents Meeting.

Hospital and boarding schools have arrangements whereby the governors can decide not to hold an Annual Parents Meeting if they consider it inappropriate.

Role of governors

All this demands a lot of work from the governors and the headteacher. Governors must prepare the report, either at a full governors meeting or in a subcommittee usually with the headteacher. They must then comment on and amend or approve the report. Finally they should attend the meeting itself.

At the meeting, governors should be prepared to answer questions about the report. The chairman should rule comments on individual teachers out of order as any complaints must go through an official procedure.

Although individual governors may not be required to speak they will gain a lot of information about what the concerns of the parents are.

- The relationship between governors and parents rests on mutual trust and communication. The governors must listen to what the parents say and the parents must trust the governors to do their best for the school.

CHECKLIST

1. Find out what the school offers in the way of social and fundraising events.

2. Ask the headteacher for a list of events such as plays or concerts for the term.

3. Contact the secretary of the PSA for a list of meetings.

4. Ask permission to attend some of these events.

5. If your school is a primary school, try to meet some of the parents in the playground before or after school.

6. Find out what the main worries of the parents are.

7. Make your own decisions about what is right for the school.

8. Discuss with the headteacher and chairman of the governors how to deal with parents' problems.

9. Take an active part in the preparation of the Annual Report to Parents.

10. Attend the Annual Parents Meeting.

11
Meeting the Experts

As a governor you will come into contact with people who are experts in their own particular field, either in education or in connected areas.

Of course, many governors are experts themselves—teachers are an obvious example—and other governors will have jobs in which they are experts.

Parent governors who do not go out to work need not feel that they are inferior. They are experts too—in their own children and their children's educational needs. They also bring their own individual common sense to the school situation.

In this chapter, however, we are concerned with the other experts you are likely to come into contact with in the course of being a governor. It is quite common for an expert invited to speak at a governors meeting to be introduced as 'This is Mr Brown, our LEA advisor' without any other explanation of Mr Brown's job. It seems to be assumed that all governors, even the new ones, know exactly what all officials do. It is a brave governor who says, 'Before we get on with the discussion, Mr Brown, please would you tell us what your job involves?' Governors are assumed to know what, for example, an EWO or HMI is. There is jargon in the world of governors as much as anywhere else and education seems to thrive on initials.

When you see in your minutes that an expert will be speaking at your next meeting, ask yourself whether you know what his or her job is. If you don't, ask the clerk or a fellow governor.

To give you a head start, here is some information about the experts you are most likely to meet.

WHO ARE THE EXPERTS?

LEA inspector/advisor
The local education authority (LEA) employs inspectors or advisors. They are not to be confused with Her Majesty's Inspectors of Schools (HMIs) who are employed by the Crown.

The LEA advisors are usually qualified teachers. Their job is to give advice on teaching arrangements, teaching methods and equipment. They also let schools know what the LEA's policy for schools is and they report back to the LEA about the school.

LEA inspectors have a responsibility towards probationary teachers. They also advise their LEA about schools and staff. They help to assess children and teachers. They appraise teachers' performance and may write teachers' references. Individual inspectors may be responsible for a particular area of education, such as computing or equal opportunities.

It is the LEA inspector who is most closely involved with individual schools and staff. Schools build up close relationships with their LEA inspectors and value their advice. It is the LEA inspector whom you will most likely meet in the course of your job as a governor because he or she will be involved in staff selection.

Her Majesty's Inspector (HMI)

HMIs are independent of governors, LEAs or schools. They are employed by the Office for Standards in Education (OFSTED) which was created separately from the DFE. OFSTED advises the Secretary of State for Education. They are under the control of the HM Chief Inspector of Schools in England (HMCI). The Welsh counterpart is the office of HM Chief Inspector of Schools in Wales (OHMCISW). HMIs inspect, report on and give advice about quality and standards of education in schools, how efficiently schools' finances are managed, and the spiritual, moral and social development of pupils. They aim to provide a full inspection of all state schools every four years.

Teams of independent inspectors bid for contracts to inspect schools from OFSTED. A summary of the inspection report must be sent to all parents. Governors must devise an action plan based on the report and send a copy to all parents. The reports are discussed by the staff so that they can see where they are being praised and what problems there are so that they can improve teaching performance and educational standards.

You are not likely to see an HMI more than once or twice in your career as a governor.

Educational Welfare Officer (EWO)

This person is sometimes known as an Educational Social Worker and that largely explains an EWO's job. EWOs liaise with social service departments and are responsible for the general well-being of school children. They are mostly known to the public as the people who chase up parents of children who are continually late or absent (the old 'truant officer' image). However, they are also around to make sure that children who need special help to attend school, such as grants, free meals, clothing or transport, get these.

EWOs also help the families of children with Special Educational Needs.

The EWOs' job means that they have to be in contact with the pupils and their families and they are therefore often based in the community rather than the Town Hall. They take time to get to know the parents and children in the local schools and can be involved in activities which bring them into contact with parents and children such as a school's Parent and Toddler Club.

An EWO can be called in by the headteacher as soon as any problem arises and their detailed knowledge of families often stops a situation getting worse.

Educational ('Child') Psychologist

All LEAs have a team of Educational Psychologists, commonly called 'child' psychologists, which is part of their Schools Psychological Service or Child Guidance Service. Educational Psychologists usually have a degree in psychology, a teaching qualification, teaching experience and specialist training.

The job of Educational Psychologists is to work with children who have behavioural or learning difficulties. They test such children and design remedial work for the child, that is, work to help the child overcome his or her difficulties and to help the child rejoin his or her age group.

Some Educational Psychologists visit schools on a regular basis so that any problems can be mentioned at these visits. Others visit at the request of the headteacher when a problem has been identified.

It is not unusual to come across an Educational Psychologist sitting in a classroom observing a particular child (unknown to the child) in order to assess his or her behaviour.

LEA officers

Officers or officials run organisations for the benefit of the public and their bosses. For example, council officers carry out decisions made by councillors. The LEA officer that you come across most will be the Clerk to the Governors, whose job has already been discussed in Chapter 5.

However, you might come across the Chief Education Officer (CEO), sometimes known as a Director of Education (DOE). He or she is directly accountable to the Council's Education Committee

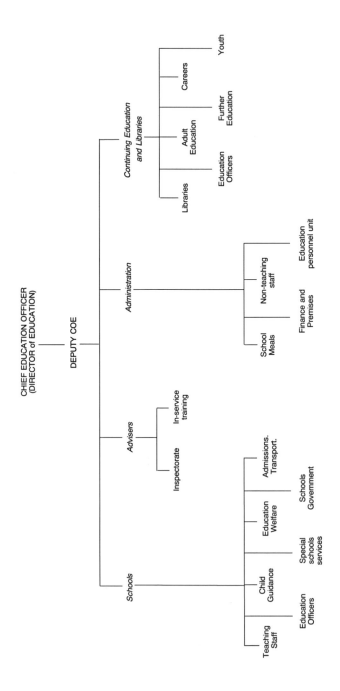

Fig. 25. Example of LEA organisation.

and is in charge of the administration needed to run the whole of the LEA's education system see Fig. 25). The CEO liaises with the Chairman of the Education Committee and the Chief Officer of other local authority departments, such as Social Services or Housing, as well as headteachers and college principals in the LEA.

Governors may well come across the CEO if he or she is called in to iron out particular problems such as the amalgamation of schools, or to address meetings of parents and governors about educational processes.

From time to time your governing body might invite other officials to address its meetings, such as the Schools Catering Officer, LEA Architect or the Council's Health and Safety Officer.

Councillors

Councillors are elected by the people in each local authority area to represent their views. They are volunteers and receive no pay, except for an allowance and travel expenses when they attend meetings.

A local authority area is divided into smaller areas, or wards. The people in these wards vote for one or more people to represent them on the council.

Your school will be in one particular ward and so you will get to know the councillor or councillors who represent you.

Councillors usually sit on subcommittees, such as Housing or Education, as well as attending the main council meeting. But even if your councillors are not on the Education committee, they can draw attention to your school's needs to the relevant councillors and officers or at a full council meeting.

Local councillors should be encouraged to visit your school to see for themselves what the problems are and what your school is achieving. They can be invited to school events and asked to address PSA or governors meetings about local education policy. A local councillor who takes an active interest in local education and knows your school well can be a great help in getting the needs of your school noticed.

Member of Parliament (MP)

Most people know that they have an MP but many are not sure who he or she is. Your MP represents a large area called a constituency. The people in that constituency vote for one person to represent them in Parliament, their MP.

Obviously your MP will be concerned with a wide area and cannot know every school intimately. Nevertheless, it is useful to invite your

MP to visit the school, perhaps on a special occasion such as a concert, so that he or she realises that your school exists.

MPs are the people to turn to if your school is involved in a campaign to 'opt out' or refuse amalgamation or simply be allowed to exist. Your MP can put pressure on the Secretary of State for Education and the LEA, present petitions to Parliament and advise parents and governors on how to present their case to the best advantage. (For more advice about campaigning see *How to Run a Local Campaign* by Polly Bird (Northcote House, 1989).)

Police

The governors have a duty to listen to the views of the local Chief of Police about any aspects of the curriculum which might be of concern to the police. The governors have to take these views into account when making any decisions about the curriculum.

This may well cause friction in some schools, usually secondary schools, where the police may be unwelcome. A few secondary schools consider that letting the police on to the school premises, even in a friendly capacity, might cause unnecessary friction between pupils, parents and police. This point of view is most prevalent in inner cities where the police are viewed as enemies outside the school.

The police have had a bad press and some headteachers have gained notoriety by forbidding police to come on to school premises, even to give talks to the children or join in school events.

Police, of course, have a right to enter school premises when pursuing a criminal or when invited to do so by the headteacher. However, there are strict codes of behaviour for when such a move is necessary and about how school children under suspicion of a crime are to be treated.

It is a pity that the unwelcoming attitude towards the police still exists in some schools. The ideal aim, of course, would be to encourage trust and respect between pupils and police so that crime is discouraged and pupils feel that they can turn to the police when they are in trouble.

Many schools, of course, do not have this negative attitude towards the police and welcome them into the school as much as possible. Police can have an important role to play in educating children and parents about road safety, personal safety, prevention of crime and so on.

Many local police stations have a home beat officer whose job involves a large amount of liaison work in the local community and who gets to know the schools in his patch very well. He or she is the first contact if there is any problem that the school would like the police to deal with. The home beat officer is also welcomed as a friend into the school and gets to know parents, pupils and governors at school events or by chatting in the playground or street.

Schools that have problems such as visitors parking outside school gates or strangers hanging around outside the school can ask their local police officer to suggest tactics. A good relationship with the police is something that the governing body should encourage.

Careers officer

All LEAs have to have a Careers Service staffed by careers officers. Careers officers travel around secondary schools to give advice to school pupils and to provide information. They act as links between secondary schools careers teachers and local employers. They usually work in area teams based in a local school and travel around the community.

THEY DON'T SCARE ME!

Well, experts often scare me, and many other governors, I suspect. Many governors regard experts of any kind, especially education experts, with awe and think that anything they say is right. This particularly applies to parent governors, especially if they are not used to meeting experts in their work or elsewhere.

Experts are people

The first thing to remember is that experts are people too, no better or worse than yourself. The only reason that they are there in front of the meeting or giving you advice is that they are experts in one particular subject which you as governors need to know about.

You are an expert too. You may well be an expert in some subject, not of immediate relevance to the meeting, but none the less useful. If you are a parent governor who stays at home you are an expert in your own child's abilities and educational needs, in bringing up children, in running a household, in juggling time about. If you don't think any of that takes expertise, then you haven't tried it!

Try to think of any expert as a friend whose advice you are asking and whose opinion you value. As with a friend's advice, you would listen carefully but make up your own mind in the end.

If you get the chance to talk to an expert informally, perhaps at a school event or outside school hours, do so. You can often learn a lot about their job and how they see it in relation to your school and what they think of the current situation.

Role of experts

Many experts are consulted by governors, headteachers or staff because they can supply information. Sometimes this is all that is needed. It is up to a governing body to listen to the information, question the expert to make sure that they have covered all the ground and then decide how best to use the information given.

On other occasions, such as at a headteacher selection meeting, advice might be given to the governing body by, for example, the LEA inspector, which the governors must then decide whether to accept, reject or modify.

Experts are available to help and advise, but unless the course of action is laid down in rules and regulations, it is the governing body who must make any final decision on any problem.

For example, an LEA advisor may recommend that a teacher should not be promoted, but it is the governors who must make that decision in the end.

Questioning the experts

It takes a lot of courage to question experts, especially if you think that the question you want to ask sounds silly or too easy.

However, if you think that you, or other governors, do not understand what has been told you, or you want to know why an expert is putting forward a particular view, then you must ask. If you don't ask you risk basing a decision on misunderstood or inadequate information or agreeing to a course of action which you disapprove of.

Remember that the expert is only an expert on that subject, not on your school. Even LEA inspectors who could be expected to know a school very well, do not always consider aspects of a problem which governors consider important.

Remember also that many governors will feel just as nervous as you about asking questions. Your question may be the one they were all longing to ask.

Write your question down and ask it as soon as you are allowed to. Don't worry if your question seems too simple. Many a child has done badly in maths, for example, because he or she failed to ask a teacher to go over a simple point again for fear of being laughed at. Don't make the same mistake. It is better to risk laughter and to get something right by understanding it, than not to ask and get it wrong. Secretly, many other governors will be pleased that you asked a question which they didn't dare to.

Questions should of course be asked through the chairman in the usual way: 'Chairman, may I ask the speaker . . .?' This makes it a bit easier to talk to any expert because you are not addressing him or her directly.

Questions can be simple, but useful, such as:

- Please would you explain that last point again?

- Please would you explain why that course of action should necessarily follow?

- Is that the only way to get that result?

- What would happen if we didn't agree to this?

- How will that affect the children/parents/staff?

- Is there an easier way of doing this?

- What do those initials mean? (You'd be surprised how many governors will listen to a speech full of jargon without understanding half of it because no one has explained what the words or initials mean.)

If you are at a bigger meeting, such as a parents meeting, and you are nervous about speaking in front of a large audience, write the question down, take some deep breaths and read it out. If you have a braver friend you could always try asking them to ask the question.

If the expert in question is very offputting, do not take it personally. You are being addressed as a governor, not an individual.

Dare to disagree

Are the experts always right? No, of course not, but you should listen carefully to what they have to say. They have experienced many times problems which you, the governor, may have met only once or twice, or not at all in connection with the school.

Bring your own common sense to what is being said and decide whether or not it is useful.

You may think that asking a question of someone who knows more than yourself about a subject is nerve-racking enough. What if you strongly disagree with what is being said?

If you have a personal experience which explains another point of view, you can use this to illustrate your opinion. If you know of another similar case which was dealt with in a different way, this too is a useful example.

Don't however, sit there without saying anything otherwise you may feel afterwards that you have been bulldozed into a course of action which you don't agree with. Disagreement should be brought out into the open so that all the governors can hear the opposing points of view and form their own opinions. A point of view different from that of the speaker might not have occurred to them.

Do not be put off by some experts' assumed exalted position. Admittedly some of them can have an offputting manner of the 'How dare you question me, I can't be wrong' type. You are entitled to disagree, as long as you do so in a reasonable manner without lapsing into personal abuse or shouting. You can disagree by saying:

- I was interested in your last point about such and such. But it seems to me that . . .

- Could you explain why you think that? I have found in a similar situation that . . . is more likely to be the case.

- Contrary to what you've been telling us, the document I read on the subject says that . . .

Don't just shout, 'That's nonsense!' (yes, it has been done) even if you are angry. You want to encourage a useful, reasoned argument which will persuade other governors to adopt your point of view, not to take part in a slanging match. Shouting at the speaker will cause the expert to clam up or shout back which will embarrass your fellow governors and not endear them to your point of view. (This applies to an argument with anyone, of course!)

- Your job as a governor is to listen to the experts, use their expertise for the good of the school, and weigh up any advice they give you so that you can make your own decisions.

- Experts are there to help you. Don't be afraid to make use of them.

CHECKLIST

1. Don't be afraid of experts; you're an expert too.

2. Experts are there to help; use them.

3. If you get a chance to talk to experts informally, do so.

4. Listen to the advice and information you are given, but make up your own mind.

5. Don't be afraid to ask questions; other governors will want to know the answers too.

6. If you want to disagree, do so, but in a reasonable manner.

12
More to Learn—How to Improve

KEEPING UP TO DATE

Education is changing so rapidly that what you know about it today may well be out of date by tomorrow. The introduction of Education Acts does not mean that Education becomes fixed from then on. Indeed, we can see by the continuing modifications to the National Curriculum that change is happening all the time.

There are two ways of making sure that you keep up to date. One is by self-teaching and the other is by attending lectures or training courses organised by other people. You may find it easier to learn by one way rather than another, but any way is better than none.

SELF-TEACHING

There are many ways in which you can keep yourself in the picture about what is happening in schools. These can include:

- television
- home-learning packs
- books
- newspapers
- specialist publications
- LEA reports
- DFE publications
- organisations

Television

All four channels produce good programmes about education in general. It is easy enough to watch the ones which seem relevant to your school situation or which cover general areas of education which governors should know about. These programmes can range from discussions to documentaries.

The Open University puts on course programmes about aspects of education for its Education Department. These are more specialised than the general television programmes and are directed at teachers. They can be on topics such as curriculum development or technology in schools. Although the programmes are often on late at night or early in the morning it can be worth the effort of watching them for a particular subject of interest. Or you could video them.

Home-learning packs

The television programmes for the Open University have already been mentioned. It is not necessary to take an Open University course in order to watch them.

The **Open University** does provide a special home-learning course for school governors as part of their Associate Student Programme. This is called *Governing Schools in the 90s: Into Action* (study pack code PE636). It can be used by a group of governors, as part of a course organised for governors, by, for example, an LEA, or by one governor working on his or her own.

The pack consists of a video, 10 workbooks and a guide for using the material in groups.

For more information about the course and the cost, contact Learning Materials Sales Office, The Open University, PO Box 188, Milton Keynes, MK7 6DH (tel: 01908 653376, or 01908 653338 out of office hours).

The BBC has produced audio cassette and workbook packs for home learning as part of its Governor Training Project:

- *Getting Started*
- *Appointing Staff*
- *Curriculum Concerns*
- *Working Partnerships*
- *Managing Resources*
- *Special Needs*

They cost £10.50 each or £57.99 for all six.

For information contact: BBC Educational Developments, PO Box 50, Wetherby, West Yorkshire, LS23 7EZ. (tel: 01937 541404).

Other organisations produce video tapes for governors, but as some of them are very expensive because they are meant to be used by groups I have not mentioned them here. Your clerk should be able to get details of them or ask at your local resource centre. You may want to get together with other governors to watch these videos and to discuss them afterwards.

Books

A list of useful books for governors (besides this one!) has been included at the end of this book. One or two which pre-date the Education Reform Act 1988 have been included because much of what they have to say is still useful.

Newspapers

All the quality daily and Sunday newspapers include articles about education either as news or as general information. However, two of the daily papers also have a day on which they provide a special section or pages on education:

- *The Guardian*—education section on Tuesday.
- *The Independent*—education section on Thursday.

Many other general magazines and newspapers carry articles on education and it is worth looking out for these.

Specialist publications

Apart from newspapers, there are many specialist publications or magazines concerned with education. Many of these are of interest and use to governors in particular. Many of them will have general articles on aspects of the education system which will be helpful and interesting. Some you could look at include:

- *The Times Educational Supplement* (weekly, 80p).

- *Child Education* (monthly, £1.75).

- *Education* (weekly, £1.30). Order from your newsagent.

- *Managing Schools Today* (6 issues; subscription is £16 a year from: The Questions Publishing Company Ltd, 6–7 Hockley Hill, Birmingham B18 5AA (tel: 0121–507 0850).

- *Junior Education* (monthly, £1.75).

Ask your library whether they get regular copies of any of the above publications or check your local resource centre.

LEA reports

Your LEA may issue special reports on aspects of education such as staffing, the curriculum or interviewing. It may also issue explanatory documents about recent education law. You should receive these from your LEA with the agenda for your next meeting. It is worth finding out from the clerk whether there are any earlier leaflets or booklets which would be of use.

DFE publications
Government publications such as the Education Acts are available from Her Majesty's Stationery Office (HMSO) at PO Box 276, London SW8 5DT. (tel: 0171–873 9090). The most recent Acts which are relevant are those of 1980, 1981, 1986, 1988, 1992 and 1993. You can also order these from your library.

The DFE produces useful information about various aspects of the Education Acts in the form of leaflets and circulars, many of which are free. For information about DFE publications contact: The Publications Despatch Centre, DFE, Honeypot Lane, Stanmore, Middlesex HA7 1AZ.

Organisations
There are a number of organisations which provide information, help, courses or helpful publications. Among the most useful are:

- National Association of Governors and Managers (NAGM), Suite 36/38, 21 Bennetts Hill, Birmingham, B2 5QP (tel: 0121–643 5787).

  This organisation works for the development and reform of school and college management. It aims to help governors to become more effective by providing information and support and by encouraging governors to talk to one another. It provides regular newsletters as well as producing papers on various aspects of being a governor. It has local branches and organises training courses and conferences.

  The subscription is £6 a year for individuals.

- Advisory Centre for Education (ACE) 1B Aberdeen Studios, 22 Highbury Grove, London N5 2EA. (tel: 0171–354 8321)

  ACE provides free advice by phone from 2–5 pm every weekday and information about state education to parents and governors. It produces many useful publications including summaries of Education Acts and a handbook for governors. A subscription costs £10 a year and includes six copies of *ACE Bulletin*

- Campaign for the Advancement of State Education (CASE), National Membership Secretary, 4 Hill Road, Carshalton, Surrey SM5 3RA.

This has local branches and campaigns to improve educational standards. It produces useful publications and individual national membership costs £3.50 a year.

- Action for Governors Information and Training (AGIT), c/o Community Education Development Council, Lyng Hall, Blackberry Lane, Coventry CV2 3JS (tel: 01203 638660).

  AGIT promotes training and support for governors by developing a working partnership between governors, parents, schools, voluntary organisations, training bodies and local authorities. It provides a national information and support service for governors and trainers. An individual subscription is £15 a year.

- Home and School Council, 81 Rustings Road, Sheffield S11 7AB (tel: 01742 662467).

  Home and School Council brings together associations concerned with the need for good home/school relations. It willingly answers a whole range of questions from concerned governors and others. It also publishes specially commissioned booklets about home/school relations, available for an annual subscription of £3.50 or individually.

- National Confederation of Parent Teacher Associations, 2 Ebbsfleet Industrial Estate, Stonebridge Road, Northfleet, Gravesend, Kent DA11 9DZ (tel: 01474 560618).

  This is the support group for PTAs. It has local groups and offers free advice and support. It can provide things such as a model constitution for a new PTA.

- National Association for Support of Small Schools, National Co-ordinator, The Cottage, Little Barningham, Norwich NR11 7LN (tel: 0126–377 553).

  This is a National Voluntary group. It provides a voice and a link for people who believe that small schools, particularly in rural areas, have important educational and social roles to perform and should be preserved. It provides information sheets and booklets. Individual membership is £5 per annum.

TRAINING COURSES

Although you can learn a lot on your own it can be more effective (and more fun!) to learn in a group with other governors. Not all governors will be able to do this because of other commitments, but if you can it is well worth while. Training provided for governors by the LEA must be free of charge.

There are several organisations which run training courses for both new and experienced governors:

- your local education authority
- your adult education institute
- outside organisations

Local Education Authority (LEA) responsibilities

According to the EA 86, your LEA must decide what training governors need in order to carry out their duties and must then provide it free of charge (see Fig. 26). The snag is, of course, that it is entirely up to the LEA what training it considers necessary—it could easily be none at all.

However, most LEAs are responding in a positive fashion to the need for improved governor training. Because there are no national guidelines, each LEA will respond to this need in a different way.

Many authorities are still in the process of evaluating, updating and organising governor training throughout their area in order to provide the high standard of training that the modern governor needs.

If training opportunities seem inadequate in your area or your LEA scheme does not seem to be providing the range of training necessary, get together with other governors and make a fuss. The more that governors demand in the way of training and information, the more they are likely to get. Governors are entitled to receive adequate training for what is a demanding job.

---

57. Every local education authority shall secure—
(a) that every governor of a county, voluntary or special school maintained by them is provided (free of charge) with—

> (i) a copy of the instrument of government and of the articles of government, for the school; and
> (ii) such other information as they consider appropriate in connection with the discharge of his functions as a governor; and

(b) that there is made available to every such governor (free of charge) such training as the authority consider necessary for the effective discharge of those functions.

Fig. 26. Information and training for governors—Education (No. 2) Act 1986. (With acknowledgement to the Controller of Her Majesty's Stationery Office.)

Ask your clerk to find out what training your authority provides. Then sign up for a course quickly—training courses are very popular.

Your authority may provide such things as:

- evening courses
- day courses (usually Saturday)
- weekend courses
- annual conferences
- governors' resource bases
- governors' support network
- governors' helpline

LEA Training Organiser

Most LEAs will have a centrally based Governor Training Organiser (or someone with a similar name) and perhaps similar officers for the separate departments in their areas. The Training Officer's job is to find out what training governors in the LEA need and to see that it is provided throughout the authority. Departmental officers will liaise with the Central Training Officer and oversee training in their own departments. In Wales, Training Officers will make sure that training is offered in English and in Welsh.

Governor training representative

Ideally each governing body should have a governor whose job is to find out what training the governing body needs, and to liaise with the clerk and training officer for the area and make sure that it is provided. Such a governor will also make sure that all members of the governing body know what training is available and get a chance to attend a course.

- If such a governor has not been appointed on your governing body or your LEA has not asked for one, why not volunteer? Governor training is too important to be left to chance.

LEA courses

Courses are provided centrally, locally or they are school-based. They can last for one session or for several sessions over a period of time. They are usually repeated at different times and at different places in the authority during the school year so that as many governors as possible get a chance to attend.

Typically courses are provided on four levels:

1. *Introduction courses*—for new governors.

2. *Follow on courses*—with sessions on the basic aspects of a governor's job such as discipline, sex education, equal opportunities and so on.

3. *Specialist courses*—on subjects such as LMS or the National Curriculum.

4. *Refresher courses*—to provide an update on basic issues.

Sometimes special courses are held for chairmen and vice-chairmen of governing bodies so that they can become more effective.

The **numbers** of governors on any one course are usually kept to no more than thirty so that everyone attending gets a chance to join in discussion groups or workshops where these are provided. When numbers are likely to be restricted, some governing bodies draw up a rota for training and send one or two governors on a course at a time. This means that every governor gets a chance to attend at least one training session.

When different governors have been on different courses it is useful to ask them to **share their experiences** with the other governors.

Apart from the benefit of the information provided on courses, it is of great help to governors to meet and talk to governors from other schools. Sharing problems and swapping advice stops governors and governing bodies feeling that they are working in isolation.

Training does not stop after one session. Because there are always new educational ideas, training is a **continuous process**. Go to as many training sessions as you can. Even if you have been to some you will need to update your experience next year. Bring back your new expertise to your governing body and encourage other governors to train too.

Annual conferences

When annual conferences are organised it is worth making the effort to get to them. They are usually at a weekend for a whole day, and at a central base. They are for all the governors in an authority or a department and may be attended by representatives of the LEA.

Governors at these conferences get a chance to raise general issues about education in their area and to exchange views with other governors. It is an opportunity to ask the authority to take action on issues of concern to governors such as training or LMS.

Resource bases

A resource base is a place where governors can find material to help them with their job as governor as well as help and advice on how to get the best from such material.

Governors need to be able to get hold of books, leaflets, videos, cassettes and home-study packs. It is possible to ask the clerk, chairman or headteacher for some of these or to approach your local library. The advantage of a resource base is that all the information is in one place, there is more of it and there are more copies of items likely to be borrowed frequently, such as home-study packs. There is also usually someone on hand to help you find the right information and to offer advice.

Resource bases can be situated in **teachers advice centres** which are locally based and already contain much of use and interest to governors. The bases can also be places for meetings and training sessions.

- Find out where your local resource base and teachers centre is. Does your LEA provide this kind of support? If not, why not ask for it?

Support network

When governors are not on training courses, how do they get to meet governors from other schools so that they can learn from their advice? Some authorities have set up governors' support networks. A co-ordinator puts governors in touch with each other or other governing bodies as well as offering help and advice.

One enlightened authority is considering listing all its governors on to a computer together with the expertise that each governor can offer to others. This will mean that individual governors can be put in touch with someone who can help them or governing bodies can contact individual governors to ask them for help and information. For example, a governor who is an accountant could be asked to advise or train another governing body on the most effective way of coping with LMS. Or a governor who needs child care could be put in touch with another governor willing to do a child swap if their governors meetings are on different days. The possibilities are endless. This is self-help training and support at its best.

All governors should be pressing their authorities to provide such a link-up service.

Governors' helpline

When the clerk or the chairman is unavailable to help with a problem, who can governors turn to? Ideally your authority should have a helpline for governors with an officer available to answer questions and give advice.

- Has your LEA got one?

The range of training opportunities and support provided by each LEA varies a great deal. It is up to governors to demand the standard of training that they need and make sure that the LEA provides it.

Adult education institute

In some areas the adult education institute (AEI) provides classes especially for governors. If these are not arranged by your LEA they will cost the same amount of money as any other adult education class in your area. If your LEA is not providing courses near you these may be a suitable alternative.

If your local adult education institute does not provide such classes it may be willing to do so if enough governors ask for them. If the request comes from several governing bodies it will carry more weight. Sometimes governors support organisations may help in organising and running such classes.

Adult education classes usually run for one evening a week for one or more terms.

Outside organisations

Several organisations either organise their own courses for governors or help LEAs or adult education institutes to organise their own classes.

The **National Association of Governors and Managers** (NAGM) has local branches and organises training courses and conferences as well as offering advice on organising training. It also provides training programmes on local radio in some areas.

The **Workers Educational Association** (WEA) has branches throughout the United Kingdom. It has no political or religious ties. It aims to respond to people's requests for education, so if a number of governors ask to arrange a course for governors it will try to do so.

If asked to do so, the WEA will try to provide people to lead courses for governors, perhaps assisted by LEA officers or advisors.

The WEA can be contacted at Temple House, 9 Upper Berkeley Street, London W1H 8BY.

GOVERNORS FROM THE ETHNIC MINORITY GROUPS

Everything that has been said about training, and indeed all aspects of the governor's job, applies to all governors.

However, governors from the ethnic minority groups are not adequately represented on many governing bodies, in spite of LEAs' attempts to attract them to the job.

This being the case, such governors may feel that they should be offered training opportunities particularly suited to their problems and needs.

LEAs have not come to terms with this need yet and special training or support groups are virtually non-existent.

Governors from the various ethnic minority groups can and do organise themselves on a local level, but this is patchy and organisation relies heavily on volunteers, so a permanent contact address is difficult to come by.

Governors who feel the need for particular help at local level should urge their LEA to provide it. Forming informal support groups is another way forward.

ONE YEAR ON

After your first year as a governor you probably feel that you have begun to understand the job a bit better but that you still have a lot to learn. Don't be put off by governors who seem to have mastered the job completely. Nobody can do that. The role of the school governor has to keep changing in order to keep up with the fast moving world of education.

If you have read this book and are acting on its advice, you:

- make regular visits to the school;

- read your papers carefully before any meeting;

- are not afraid to ask questions to ensure that you understand an issue clearly;

- keep in contact with the parents;

- attend training courses when you can;

- discuss problems with fellow governors and are not afraid to ask for advice when you need it.

If you are doing this and you care about your school you are doing your best for the children in the school. Doing your best to ensure that the school provides the best education possible for the children in it is what being a governor is all about.

Remember that your contribution is important and is needed by your school. Confidence will come in time and one day you will find that new governors are turning to you for advice!

CHECKLIST

1. Find out what you can learn in your own time from television, newspapers, LEA reports, DFE publications and governors organisations.

2. Find out what home-learning schemes are available.

3. Ask your clerk what LEA training courses are available in your area.

4. Make sure your governing body has a governor training representative.

5. If training is inadequate in your area get the governing body to ask for more.

6. Attend as many training courses as possible.

7. Keep up to date by attending new or refresher courses.

8. Join a governors' network scheme or get one organised.

9. Find out which other organisations in your area provide governor training.

10. Find out where your nearest governor resource base is—and use it!

11. Ethnic minorities—find out if there is a local support group.

12. Be confident that you are needed on your governing body and are making a worthwhile contribution.

Glossary

Advisor (Inspector) Local authority officer who gives advice and support, and arranges training for teachers in schools.

Aided school Voluntary school for which the trustees provide the building and the LEA pays for staff and internal maintenance.

Articles of Government Document telling governors their powers and duties.

Attainment targets Group of learning skills or facts needed to understand a subject.

Baker Days Five days compulsory in-service training for practising teachers. Named after Kenneth Baker, previously Secretary of State for Education and Science.

Banding Putting pupils of similar ability in the same teaching group.

CCTA (City College for the Technology of the Arts) State-aided school independent of LEA, with an emphasis on arts technologies.

CDT Craft, design and technology

CEO Chief Education Officer or County Education Officer. Sometimes called a Director of Education.

Controlled school Voluntary school, usually run by a church. All costs are paid by the LEA.

Core curriculum A group of subjects followed by all pupils.

Core subjects English, Maths and Science within the National Curriculum.

County school School owned and maintained by the LEA.

CTC (City Technology College) State-aided school independent of LEA, with an emphasis on technology.

DFE Department for Education.

Educational Psychologist Expert who works with children who have behavioural or learning difficulties.

ERA Education Reform Act 1988.

EWO (Educational Welfare Officer) Educational social worker responsible for the well-being of school children.

Exclusion Temporary, indefinite or permanent barring of a pupil from school.

Ex-officio By virtue or because of office. For example, a headteacher is an ex-officio governor.

Family grouping *See* vertical grouping.

Foundation subjects Technology, history, geography, art, music, PE and a modern foreign language within the National Curriculum.

GCSE (General Certificate of Secondary Education) The main secondary school exams taken at sixteen.

Grant-maintained school School which has 'opted-out' of LEA control and is financed directly by the government.

HMI (Her Majesty's Inspector) Independent inspector employed by OFSTED to inspect educational institutions and monitor national education standards and trends.

Incentive allowance Extra payments to teachers for special responsibility, quality teaching, filling a difficult post or teaching a shortage subject.

In-service training Courses to enable practising teachers to update their skills.

INSET In-service Education and Training of Teachers.

Instrument of Government Constitution and rules of a governing body.

Key Reporting Stages Ages 7, 11, 14 and 16 when pupils are assessed on attainment targets for those stages.

LEA Local Education Authority.

LMS (Local Management of Schools) The delegation of financial control to schools.

Main grade Pay scale for all teachers except headteacher and deputy headteacher.

Maintained school School for which the LEA takes financial and administrative responsibility.

Multicultural education Education to ensure that all children are aware of and sensitive to the many different ethnic cultures in our society.

National Curriculum Basic curriculum as set out in the Education Reform Act 1988.

OFSTED Office for Standards in Education.

PE Physical education.

Probationary teacher Teacher completing the first year of practical work in school as a qualified teacher to prove his or her proficiency.

Profiles Groups of Attainment Targets, which are themselves groups of learning skills and facts.

PTA Parent Teacher Association. Nowadays often called Parent Staff Association (PSA).

Pupil-teacher ratio Number of pupils in a school divided by the number of teaching staff giving the number of pupils theoretically taught by each teacher. In an individual class, the number of pupils a teacher actually has.

Qualified teacher A teacher who has completed a recognised course of initial training and has been approved as qualified by the DES.

RE Religious education.

SAT (Standard Assessment Task) Activities designed to find out what level each child is at in National Curriculum subjects.

Secular education Everything taught in school except religious education.

SEN (Special Educational Needs) A child is said to have special needs if he or she has a learning difficulty needing special educational provision.

Special Agreement school One of a few Voluntary schools, mostly Catholic, for which the LEA has paid most of the cost of a new building.

Special school Maintained school providing facilities for children with serious or long-term special educational needs.

Statement of special educational needs Children with severe difficulties are given a 'statement of special educational needs' describing the child's needs and the educational provision required.

Supply teacher Temporary teacher who takes a class when the class teacher is away.

Tertiary education Education after the age of 16. Either 16–19 or including adult education.

Vertical grouping Primary school class containing children of different ages. Sometimes called 'family grouping'.

Virement Transfer of money from one heading to another in a financial budget.

Voluntary school School built by a voluntary body. Largely financed by the LEA but retaining a large measure of control. (*See* Aided, Controlled and Special Agreement schools.)

Useful Addresses

Action for Governors Information and Training (AGIT), c/o Community Education Development Council, Lyng Hall, Blackberry Lane, Coventry CV2 3JS (tel: 01203 44814).

Advisory Centre for Education (ACE) 1B Aberdeen Studios, 22, Highbury Grove, London N5 2EA (tel: 0171–354 8321).

BBC Educational Developments, PO Box 50, Wetherby, West Yorkshire LS23 7EZ (tel: 01937 541404).

Campaign for the Advancement of State Education (CASE), 158 Durham Road, London SW20 0DG (tel: 0181–944 8206).

Centre for Continuing Education, 12–14 Claremont, University of Bradford, Bradford BD7 1BG.

Child Education, Scholastic Publications Ltd., Villiers House, Clarendon Avenue, Leamington Spa, Warwickshire CV32 5PR (tel: 01926 887 799; Fax: 01926 883331).

The City Technology Colleges Trust, 15 Young Street, London W8 5E8 (tel: 0171–376 2511).

Department for Education (DFE) Hdqtrs, Sanctuary Building, Great Smith Street, London SW1P 3BT (tel: 0171–925 5000).

DFE Helpline, East Cross Centre, Waterden Road, London E15 (tel: 0181–533 2000).

Department of Education for Northern Ireland, Rathgael House, Baloo Road, Bangor, Co. Down BT19 2PR (tel: 01247–270077).

DFE Publications, The Publications Despatch Centre, Honeypot Lane, Canons Park, Stanmore, Middlesex HA7 1AZ. (tel: 0171–952 2366 X325/503/737).

Education, 21–7 Lamb's Conduit Street, London WC1N 3NJ (tel: 0171–242 2548; fax: 0171–831 2855).

Education Today, Longman Group UK Ltd., 6th Floor, Westgate House, The High, Harlow, Essex CM20 1YR (tel: 01279–442 601; fax: 01279–444501).

Equal Opportunities Commission, Overseas House, Quay Street, Manchester M3 3HN (tel: 0161–833 9244).

The Grant-Maintained Schools Foundation, 36 Great Smith Street, London SW1P 3BU (tel: 0171–233 4666).

The Guardian, 119 Farringdon Road, London EC1R 3ER (tel: 0171–278 2332; fax: 0171–837 2114/833 8342).

Health Education Authority—School Governors' Project, Warren House, Merrion, Castle Martin, Dyfed SA71 5HR.

Her Majesty's Stationery Office, PO Box 276, London SW8 5DT (tel orders: 0171–873 9090; tel enquiries: 0171–973 0011).

Home and School Council, 81 Rustings Road, Sheffield S11 7AB (tel: 01142 662467).

The Independent, 40 City Road, London EC1Y 2DB (tel: 0171–253 1222; fax: 0171–956 1581).

The Institute of Chartered Accountants in England and Wales (ICAEW), PO Box 433, Chartered Accountants Hall, Moorgate Place, London EC2P 2BJ (tel: 0171–628 7060).

Junior Education, Scholastic Publications Ltd., Villiers House, Clarendon Avenue, Leamington Spa, Warwickshire CV32 5PR. (tel: 01926 887799 fax: 01926 883331).

Managing Schools Today, The Questions Publishing Company Ltd, 6–7 Hockley Hill, Hockley, Birmingham B18 5AA (tel: 0121 507 0850; fax: 0121–554 7513).

The National Association for Primary Education (NAPE), 60 Willett Way, Petts Wood, Kent BR5 1QE (tel: 01689 29971).

National Association for Support of Small Schools, National Coordinator, The Cottage, Little Barningham, Norwich NR11 7LN (tel: 0126 377 553).

National Association of Governors and Managers (NAGM), Suite 36/38, 21 Bennetts Hill, Birmingham B2 5QP (tel: 0121–643 5787).

National Confederation of Parent Teacher Associations, 2 Ebbsfleet Industrial Estate, Stonebridge Road, Northfleet, Gravesend, Kent DA11 9DZ (tel: 01474 560618).

National Curriculum Council, 15–17 New Street, York, YO1 2RA (tel: 01909 652533).

National Federation for Education Research, The Mere, Upton Park, Slough, Berkshire SL1 2DQ (tel: 01753 74123).

The Open University, Learning Materials Sales Office, PO Box 188, Milton Keynes MK7 6DH (tel: 01908 653376, or 0908 653338 outside office hours).

Reading and Language Information Centre, University of Reading, Bulmershe Court, Earley, Reading RG6 1HY (tel: 01734 318820).

School Examinations and Assessment Council (SEAC), Information Centre, Newcombe House, 45 Notting Hill Gate, London W11 3LQ (tel: 0171–229 1234).

Scottish Education Department, New St. Andrew's House, Edinburgh EH1 3TG (tel: 0131–556 8400).

The Times Educational Supplement, Priory House, St John's Lane, London EC1M 4BX (tel: 0171–253 3000; fax: 0171–251 4698).

The Welsh Office Education Department, Cathays Park, Cardiff CF1 3NQ (tel: 01222 825111).

Workers Educational Association, Temple House, 9 Upper Berkeley Street, London W1H 8BY.

Further Reading

Citrine's ABC of Chairmanship, eds: Michael Cannell & Norman Citrine (NCLC Publishing Society Ltd., 1992).

Education A–Z, Elizabeth Wallis (ACE, 5th edition, 1991).

Education Act 1980 (HMSO, 1980).

Education Act 1981 (HMSO, 1981).

Education Act 1993 (HMSO, 1993).

The Education Fact File, June Statham & Donald Mackinnon with Heather Cathcart (Hodder & Stoughton, 2nd edition, 1991).

Education (No. 2) Act 1986 (HMSO, 1986).

Education Reform Act 1988 (HMSO, 1988).

Education Reform Act: Local Management of Schools (DES circular No. 7/8/8, 6 September 1988).

Education Re-formed. A Guide to the Education Reform Act, Stuart Maclure (Hodder & Stoughton, 2nd edition, 1989).

Education (Schools) Act 1992 (HMSO, 1992).

Getting Ready for Change—A Guide to LMS for governors, leaflet (produced by Coopers & Lybrand for NAGM, 1989).

Governors Handbook (ACE, 1988).

Governors Reports and Annual Parents Meeting: The 1988 Act and Beyond (National Foundation for Educational Research, 1988).

A Guide to Governing Schools, D. Harding (Paul Chapman Publishing, 1988).

A Guide to the National Curriculum, Bob Moon (OUP, 1991).

How to Conduct Staff Appraisals, Nigel Hunt (How To Books, 2nd edition 1994).

How to Know Your Rights: Students, Shirley Meredeen (How To Books, 1991).

How to Know Your Rights: Teachers, Neil Adams (How To Books, 1991).

How to Manage Budgets & Cash Flows, Peter Taylor (How To Books, 1994).

How to Manage People at Work, John Humphries (How To Books, 1992).

How to Run a Local Campaign, Polly Bird (Northcote House/How To Books, 1989).

How to Understand Finance at Work, Peter Marshall (How To Books, 1994).

Local Financial Management in Schools, ed. P. Downes (Blackwell, 1988).

Local Management of Schools, An Introduction for Teachers, Governors and Parents, Brent Davies & Chris Braund (Northcote House, 1989).

Managing the Primary School Budget, Brent Davies & Linda Ellison (Northcote House, 1990).

School Governors, Keith Anderson, David Cook & Tony Saunders (Society of Education Officers/Longman, 3rd edition 1992).

The School Governor's Handbook, Martin Leonard (Blackwell, 1989).

School Governors: How to Become a Grant-Maintained School (DES, 1988).

The School Governor's Legal Guide, Chris Low (Croner Publications, 4th edition, 1992).

Schools, Parents and Governors: A New Approach to Accountability, Joan Sallis (Routledge, 1988).

Shouldn't You Become a School Governor? (DES, 1988).

Summary of Education Act 1986, Joan Sallis (ACE, 1986).

Summary of Education Act 1988, Joan Sallis (ACE, 1988).

The Sunday Times. The National Curriculum: A guide for parents, Charles Hyams (Chapmans, 1993).

You are the Governor. How to be Effective in Your Local School, Barbara Bullivant (Bedford Square Press, 2nd edition, 1989).

• Organisations such as the National Association for Governors and Managers (NAGM), Advisory Centre for Education (ACE) and Action for Governors Information and Training (AGIT) produce useful publications and leaflets. Write to them for information.

Index